A TIME
TO
LISTEN

Jack R. Reed, Jr.

A TIME TO LISTEN

The Building Blocks of One Man's
Personal Theology and Philosophy

JACK R. REED, JR.

gatekeeper press™
Columbus, Ohio

A Time To Listen: The Building Blocks of One Man's Personal Theology and Philosophy

Published by Gatekeeper Press
2167 Stringtown Rd, Suite 109
Columbus, OH 43123-2989
www.GatekeeperPress.com

The editorial work for this book is entirely the product of the author. Gatekeeper Press did not participate in and is not responsible for any aspect of this element.

ISBN (hardcover): 9781662909986
ISBN (paperback): 9781662909993

For my wife Lisa
And for my daughter Kirk, my son Jack, and their families

Select and collect all those words and sentences that in all your reading have been to you like the blast of a trumpet out of Shakespeare, Seneca, Moses, John, and Paul.

—Ralph Waldo Emerson

Preface

For almost 50 years I have been taking notes in my Bible since I purchased it as my Old Testament textbook at Vanderbilt University in the spring of 1973. I believe it has become the most valuable gift I can pass down to my two children. It contains the building blocks of my theology and my philosophy, taken from hours of listening to sermons, Sunday School lessons, lay academies, and other classes I've attended at First United Methodist Church here in my hometown of Tupelo, Mississippi.

I never intended these notes to be published, but I have two children and one Bible. I spent a year copying these personal "annotations" by hand onto index cards. Our local printer then made two copies and bound them in a spiral binder for my children. Then—surprisingly—friends and family heard about the collection and requested copies. After several renditions of this, I have decided to have them more professionally bound.

The annotations more or less follow the books of the Bible, but often include thoughts that I simply wanted to remember.

When I could, I credited the pastors and teachers I heard speak them at the time. Some of the entries are my own, inspired by what I was hearing. Some are from books or texts I read. Any errors in attribution are mine alone.

In rereading the entries for this project, I am not surprised that many of them call me to be an instrument for social justice (Micah 6.8), to be a Good Samaritan, to adopt the fruits of the Spirit, and to support my personal mission statement—God wants life to be a party. It's just up to us to make sure everyone is invited. (I believe I heard that, or something close to it, from pastor Tony Campolo.)

I also tried to include very practical, though profound, thoughts to help me and my children navigate the journey of our lives; for example, "To forgive is to be powerful"; and "There are enough sad times in life. Make sure we enjoy and celebrate the good times."

In closing, I am humbled and recognize the enormous blessings I have received in my life: my wife Lisa and our children, Kirk and Jack, and grandchildren, my parents, brother and sisters, our friends, these spiritual mentors, my church family. I hope this collection will be a blessing to those of you who read them. Perhaps what began as a personal effort will help all of us to remember to live with a wider circle of love and compassion, for we, after all, are all God's children.

God bless you,

Jack Reed, Jr.

A Time To Listen

1. "God wants life to be a party. It's just up to us to make sure that everyone is invited."

> (My personal mission statement)
> (Per Tony Campola)

2. Light.

"Light plays a major part in the Bible and in our everyday lives. Light is one of the most comforting words in the English language. It helps us see during times when we couldn't otherwise, it gives us warmth, and reveals the truth to us.

When Jesus was sent into the world, he was sent into a world of darkness and sin to help people see the real truth and give protection to all. So, Jesus, like light, will always be there for us in times of darkness to give off warmth, protection, and to reveal the way to all who ask.

> Kirk Reed Forrester
> (12-6-94)

3. The poem from the book

The Other Wise Man by Henry Van Dyke.

"Who seeks for heaven alone to save his soul,
May keep the path, but will not reach the goal;

While he who walks in love may wander far,
Yet God will bring him where the blessed are."

4.   "Aim high and consider yourself worthy of great things."

R. W. Reed Sr.'s motto

5.   Theology:

"I don't believe we can "fall from grace." That would be limiting God.

Rev. Cliff Davis

6.   From *The Gospel goes to Broadway* sermon series

"The Impossible Dream"

Don Quixote saw only the best in people.
He was idealistic.
God wants to give us a dream of what we can be.
Don Quixote saw "Dulcinea" within "Aldonza".
Jesus saw a different Mary Magdalene, a different Peter.

Rev. Jim McCormick

7.   From *The Gospel goes to Broadway* sermon series.

"Wouldn't It Be Loverly" – sung by Eliza Doolittle

- Eliza wants a relationship.
- He who dies with the most toys doesn't win, in fact, one who tries to get the most toys has already died.
- What kind of person do you bring to the circumstances you confront?

- The size of your life is determined by the decision you make on following the goal of making you happy.
- What you put in your heart is more important than what we put in our minds or on our lips.

Rev. Jim McCormick

8. Where your ability intersects with the world's needs ... there is God's call for you.

Rev. B. F. Lee

9. Abraham Lincoln:

A minister approached President Lincoln during the Civil War and said, "I sure hope God is on our side". Lincoln responded, "I'm not worried about that. I just pray that I and our nation are on God's side."

(That's the side we always want to be on.)

10. Our worship ought to make a difference in the way we live.

11. Greatness is having the right values and living up to them.

12. Don't forget to create time for the CREATOR today.

13. <u>The Church</u>.

The <u>first</u> responsibility of the Christian community is to affirm to people that they are the sons and daughters of God.

14. "As a person thinks in his (her) heart, so shall he (she) be."

    Anonymous

15. <u>Everybody</u> needs to feel validated, affirmed, worthy, capable, loved, hugged, cared about, special.

16. Every life needs to have a storm shelter.

17. Prayer is thanks and hope.

18. Throughout history there have been those who have made a stand, and there have been those who stood idly by, lazily, uncaringly.

19. No one knows where destiny ends and freedom begins. Yet we are all responsible for our own behavior and we are accountable for it.

    "Destiny" includes heredity, home, environment, social setting, teachers.

    Rev. Cliff Davis

20. God's love is not just a pillow to sleep on; it is a stepping stone from which to step onto from which to live a complete life.

21. "All that we are is God's gift to us; all that we become is our gift to God."

22. Our Christian faith does not give us a way to get <u>around</u> events in life, but rather a way to <u>get</u> <u>through</u> events and personal crises.

23. There is no personal holiness without social holiness.

John Wesley

24. <u>The</u> Church.

   There is no other institution in our society that exists to be a means of grace to each other.

25. To whom much is given, much is expected. To whom much is forgiven, much is expected.

26. <u>Love</u> is a verb.
   Love is something you do, not something you feel.

27. Relationships – and their quality – determine the quality of our lives and our families' lives and our community's.

   Togetherness.

28. <u>Genesis</u>.

   We do not inherit sin from Adam and Eve.
   We <u>do</u> inherit our human nature.
   We each have the freedom to choose our paths.
   I am my own Adam.

Rev. Cliff Davis

29. <u>Genesis</u>.

   "The Fall".

   By misusing their freedom Adam and Eve became separated from God, separated from one another; separated from their better nature.

Sin is separation; it is alienation. Sin can be forgiven, but consequences remain.

30. Genesis.

Noah lived in a time of many problems, but he became a part of the answer, not part of the problem.

"I can't solve America's immorality, but I can be moral myself. I can be part of the answer."

Rev. Cliff Davis

31. Genesis. Jacob & Esau.

During most of his life Jacob wanted to have everything and to have it now. But he encounters God – wrestles with him – grace comes – he gets a new name, Israel.

Then, in one of the greatest moments of the Bible, he receives grace from his brother Esau.

(The best example of grace in the Old Testament.)

32. Genesis. Noah and the Flood.

The rainbow is a sign of God's covenant with man.

(I saw a beautiful double rainbow shortly after my mother died. I now think of her whenever I see one. A sweet memory. – Jack Reed, Jr.)

33. When we deserve love the least, we need it the most.

34. At a particular moment in time and place, we are the best God has to offer in that situation.

35. "People who are at war with themselves, often make casualties of the ones they love."

Rev. Fred Craddock

36. Exodus.

Abraham is looked upon as the Father of the Hebrew people, but Moses is looked upon as the Father of the Hebrew religion.

37. Exodus & Moses.

Moses was the dominant figure of the Old Testament. He led the exodus out of Egypt; he brought down the Law from Mt. Sinai; he kept the covenant. Yet before he began, he was remarkably like us – an unremarkable man, not yet a leader. And he was quite humble as he tried to avoid service. But God said, "I will be with you." And He gave him some help (his brother Aaron).

38. Passover & Communion.

The Jews remember the Passover as a sign of God's favor and covenant.

For Christians Holy Communion is a time to remember and "re-member", to join our people together again and to re-connect us to Jesus, and to God, and to His power.

39. The <u>Sabbath</u>.

The Sabbath should not be merely a time to sleep but rest, think, study, consider religious ideas, worship, spend time with family, with friends, prayer, reflection, thought. A regular time.

Rev. Cliff Davis

40. The <u>Sabbath</u>.

Going to church on Sundays recharges my batteries to be the kind of person that I want to be.

I always feel better having gone. Inspired by the music. Seeing Lisa in the choir. Being with friends, family. Tradition worth keeping.

Jack Reed, Jr.

41. Our church is a gift from those who went before us.

42. People long to be acknowledged.

43. Re: Moses not making it to the "Promised Land".

"Moses simply died before they got to the Promised Land; but in early times the Hebrews figured that <u>if</u> something happened <u>then</u> God made it happen and his reason must have been (something)."

Rev. Jim McCormick

44. <u>Joshua</u> <u>24:15</u>.

   "And if you be unwilling to serve the Lord, choose this day whom you will serve … but as for me and my house, we will serve the Lord."

   <u>Not</u> choosing to do the Lord's work here on Earth <u>is</u> making a choice.

   Jack Reed, Jr.

45. Ships are safe in the harbor; but that is not what they were built for.

   (1st heard at Camp Mondamin)

46. Our role is to be an agent of faithful, courageous hope in the world.

47. <u>Free</u> <u>will</u>.

   "We are free to choose what we do, but we are not free to choose the consequences."

   Rev. Cliff Davis

48. <u>The Book of Ruth</u>.

   One point of the Book:

   One need not be a Jew to be a child of God.

49. <u>The Book of Ruth</u>.

If King David is indeed descended from a mixed marriage, then the qualities of mercy and love trump purity of bloodline.

Rev. Roy Ryan

50. "Charity is no substitute for justice witheld."

    - Saint Augustine

51. Diedrich Bonnehoffer:

    "Love doesn't hold marriage together. Marriage holds love together."

    We need the structure to support us.

52. We become, at our best, the embodiment, passionate expression of God's love on earth.

53. God's love is a light which shines both into our heart and into the world.

    It disperses gloom and darkness.

54. Isaiah 58:6-9.

    Mission is inherent in discipleship. Disciple is also a verb. Disciples disciple.

    To be the salt of the earth we must get out of the shaker to be effective.

    We've got to turn our light on – to touch the lives of people around us.

One's relationship to his fellows reveals one's relationship to God.

55. Isaiah 40:30-31. Great verses!

    30) "Even youths shall faint and be weary, and young men shall fall exhausted;

    31) but they who wait for the Lord
    shall renew their strength,
    they shall mount up with wings like eagles,
    they shall run and not be weary,
    they shall walk and not faint."

56. In the Bible there are two kinds of time:

    times of preparation
    times of action.

    Isaiah was preparing the Jews for their deliverance.
    (In our lives we need times of preparation before our times of action as well.)

    Christians have read into Isaiah that all of God's people, not just the Jews, would be delivered.

57. 1 Samuel 3:4.

    "Then the Lord called, 'Samuel! Samuel!' and he said, "Here I am!"

    This verse's language provides the lyrics for my favorite hymn "Here I am Lord." Its message is inspirational.

58. <u>1 Samuel 17</u>. (The story of David and Goliath.)

Saul's weapons offered to David did not fit David. So, David used his own strength and abilities to slay the giant.

Point: Be ourselves. Use our own weapons to fight today's "giants", and claim God's powerful help when we are trying to do God's will. For <u>we</u> are the hands of God today, in today's world.

59. <u>2 Samuel 2:24</u>.

"Ye daughters of Israel, weep over Saul …"

In order to redeem our loses we must:
1) Name the grief and take time to cry;
2) Look for God's grace (in others, in the world);
3) Allow the love of God to lead you, in time, to the love of life.

60. <u>2 Samuel 3:38.</u> "Do you not know that a prince and a great man has fallen this day...?" (This verse spoken at our friend Jimmy Webb's funeral)

61. <u>1 Kings 8</u>. (The dedication of the temple in Jerusalem.)

Upon the 100th Anniversary of our sanctuary
FUMC Tupelo, Mississippi
January 23, 2000.

"How many lives have been transformed within these church walls!"

Bishop Jack Meador

Coming to services every Sunday in our sanctuary recharges my own batteries to do the work of the world Monday-Saturday. The music, the sermons, the friends, the sense of reverence.

Jack Reed, Jr.

62. Have you heard the voice of God in this church?

Yes.

When I join the congregation in singing hymns.
When I am moved by the music of the Chancel Choir.
When I am moved by the children's choir (particularly when Kirk & Jack were singing).
When I am inspired by a great sermon.
When I am in prayer.

Jack Reed, Jr.

63. 1 Kings 19:11-12.

"... but the Lord was not in the wind, ... nor the earthquake, ... nor the fire; and after a still small voice."

Also translated   "a sheer silence"
                   "a light whisper"
                   "the sound of a soft breath"

One point: "If we are always in loud places, we (may) will miss God's message to us. We might miss the birth of a baby in a stall or a resurrection in a garden."

Rev. Andy Ray

64. <u>1 Kings 19:11-12</u>.

"… a sheer silence."

"God doesn't speak to me either.
Jesus Christ is the Word of God.
The life of Jesus is our word.
Don't believe you must have heard God's voice directly to you beyond Jesus, in order to believe."

Rev. Cliff Davis

65. <u>1 Kings 19:11-12</u>.

"a still small voice" or "a sheer silence"

Mother Theresa: "When I pray, I just listen."

Q. What does God say?

A. "He just listens."

66. <u>2 Kings 2:9</u>.

And Eli'sha said, "I pray you, let me inherit a double share of your spirit."

A Father's Legacy. (And a Mother's)

(To try to give your children the things money can't buy: love, compassion, humor, generosity, a free spirit, character, respect for others, kindness, courage, loyalty, reverence)

67. Nehemiah 12:27.

"... to celebrate the dedication with gladness, with thanksgiving and with singing, with cymbals, harps, and lyres."

Seeing Lisa in the Chancel Choir for all of our adult lives and hearing the Choir weekly an on the great Holy Days of the church – these have meant so much to my life and to my faith journey. I am grateful for our music, and for the inspirational leadership of Beverly McAlilly!

68. The Book of Job.

When you are faced with a belief decision, ask yourself two questions:

1. Is it reasonable?

2. Is it helpful? Or harmful?

Rev. Cliff Davis

69. The Book of Job.

No one completely understands another.

Communication (in marriage, friendship, family) represents an attempt to understand.

There is a difference between <u>hearing</u> a friend and <u>listening</u> to a friend.

Listening implies considering and trying to understand.

Listen as hard as you want to speak.

70. <u>The Book of Job</u>.

"When you need love the most, is when you deserve it the least."

"When you need a friend the most, is when you deserve it the least."

Jack Reed, Jr.

71. <u>The Book of Job</u>.

Early on Job's <u>memory</u> of good times, of some high and holy moments which he can remember to see him through, helped him. <u>Memory</u> is like a <u>night-light</u> which helps us see through the <u>darkness</u> of the low times.

Take time to write down the good times – save photographs – to review when low times come.

72. <u>The Book of Job</u>.

Per Rev. Cliff Davis

"Leslie Weatherhead once said, upon seeing an insect crawl across the pulpit, 'We understand God about as well as the insect understands me.'

Immanuel Kant: "The finite cannot understand the infinite."

73. The Book of Job.

Because we feel God is absent does not mean that God is absent.

Dr. Alyce McKenzie

74. The Book of Job.

Re his friends:

Know when to ignore bad advice.

75. Imagine if we coveted God's purposes for our world.

76. The Book of Job.

"Job's capacity for articulate complaint exceeds his reputation for patience."

"Job is a story told to illustrate a truth. That truth is that the righteous do suffer; and yet God will take care of you in your suffering. Not prevent the suffering but take care of you."

Rev. Cliff Davis

77. The Book of Job.

"There must be a place in one's belief which allows for the time of the storm. The Providence of God does not relieve us from the realities of the world."

Rev. Cliff Davis

(Whose own son, Dwayne, committed suicide.)

78. The Psalms.

"The Psalms have something for everybody. Every prayer here is not Christian; so, when you come to something like 'God slay my enemies' just skip it and go on, because there are many precious jewels of thoughts and words in The Psalms."

Rev. Cliff Davis

79. Psalm 8.

God believes in us.

We need to believe that.

Each of us is a unique miracle in the mind of God.

God has a beautiful dream (idea) of what each of us will become.

80. Psalm 8.

There is a divine spark in each of us. God believes in us.

Parents should spend our time building our children up, not pointing out their deficiencies.

81. Psalm 16. (A Psalm of trust and confidence in God.)

Verse 11: "Thou dost show me the path of life; in thy presence there is fulness of joy, in thy right hand are pleasures for ever more."

18

The New Testament called followers of Jesus "The Way". I like these images, "on the path", following "the Way". Life is a journey not a destination.

Jack Reed, Jr.

82. Psalm 19:5.

"... like a strong man runs his course with joy."

(This is an image I aspire to in describing my life.)

Jack Reed, Jr.

83. Psalm 19:14.

"Let the words of my mouth and the meditation of my heart be acceptable in thy sight,

O Lord,

my rock

and my redeemer."

84. Psalm 22:1.

"My God, my God, why has thou forsaken me?"

(Jesus quoted these words on the cross.) (Mark 15:34)

Despair at times in our lives can be real.

Questioning God can be real. (See Job.)

We just can't "camp there". (Rev. Cliff Davis)

The next psalm is Psalm 23. We look for the light at the end of the tunnel. There is light there.

85. Psalm 23.

"The Lord is my shepherd, I shall not want;
He makes me lie down in green pastures,
He leads me beside still waters; he restores my soul,
He leads me in paths of righteousness for his name sake.

Even though I walk through the valley of the shadow of death,
I fear no evil;
For thou art with me;
thy rod and thy staff, they comfort me.

Thou preparest a table before me
In the presence of my enemies;
Thou anointest my head with oil,
My cup overflows.

Surely goodness and mercy shall follow me all the days of my life;
And I shall dwell in the house of the Lord forever."

86. Psalm 23.

This Psalm inspired the sublime music "My Shepherd Will Supply My Needs" which contains this most poignant verse –

"no more a stranger or a guest, but like a child at home."

What more comforting image – both to me as a child in our home growing up, or as a parent with Lisa welcoming Kirk and Jack and their families back home!

87. <u>Psalm 23</u>.

Whenever we are personally walking through our darkness (when our loved ones, or we ourselves, are facing the shadow of death):

<u>we</u> <u>do</u> <u>not</u> <u>walk</u> <u>alone</u>.

God is with us.

This is one of very foundational building blocks of my faith.

Jack Reed, Jr.

88. <u>Psalm 24</u>.

Psalm 24:1 "The earth is the Lord's and the fulness thereof, the world and those who dwell therein."

A great psalm.

"We are only tenants in this world, and yet we act like we own the place."

Also,

"I can't think of any greater privilege than to be given the task of accepting God's purposes in His world."

Rev. Jim McCormick

89. <u>Psalm 24:3</u>.

"Who shall ascend the hill of the Lord?

And who shall stand in his holy place?"

"Religion is not a separate part of life, it <u>is</u> life.

To be holy means to be "wholly" God's.

Rev. Jim McCormick

90. <u>Psalm 24</u>.

<u>Happiness</u> is a <u>by-product</u> of a larger mission in life. <u>Happiness</u> comes only from being a good steward of what we have to give back.

91. <u>Psalm 27</u>.

(This Psalm was the scripture read in our church the Sunday after the "Attack on America 9-11-01", September 16, 2001.)

"The Lord is my light and my salvation; whom shall I fear?

The Lord is the stronghold of my life; of whom shall I be afraid?"

Sermon: "The love of God is <u>expressed</u> through service."

92. <u>Psalm 30:5</u>.

"… Weeping may tarry for the night, but joy comes in the morning."

Remember in times of trouble that the sun shall rise tomorrow. Life will go on.

93. Psalm 32:5.

"I acknowledge my sin to thee and I do not hide my iniquity;
I said, "I will confess my transgressions to the Lord".
and then thou didst forgive the guilt of my sin.

"New beginnings". We all make mistakes.

There is a direct relationship between spiritual health and mental health and physical health.

Asking forgiveness and forgiving are both sometimes hard to do and are essential to lasting relationships and mutual respect.

94. Psalm 37. (Abraham Lincoln's favorite psalm.)

Selected verses:

37:3 "Trust in the Lord, and do good."

37:8 "Refrain from anger, and forsake wrath! Fret not yourself…"

37:11 "… the meek shall posses the land, and delight themselves in abundant prosperity."

37:25 "I have been yours, and now am old; yet I have not seen the righteous forsaken or his children begging bread.

37:26 "He is ever giving liberally and lending and his children become a blessing."

95. Psalm 46:1-3.

"God is our refuge and strength, a very present help in trouble, therefore we will not fear though the earth should change, though the mountains shake in the heart of the sea; though its waters roar and foam, though the mountains tremble with its tumult."

The words of one of my favorite anthems sung by our Chancel Choir. Powerful assertion of God's might.

46:8 "Come behold the works of the Lord..."

96. Psalm 46:10.

"Be still, and know that I am God."

97. Psalm 51:10.

"Create in me a clean heart, O God, and put a new and right spirit within me."

This, perhaps, anticipates the New Testament's declaration of the Holy Spirit, that we Christians rely upon as part of the Trinity, with God and Jesus.

Today the Holy Spirit is a reassuring part of our faith in our own journeys.

Jack Reed, Jr.

98. <u>Psalm 63</u>.

This Psalm was read on the 100th Anniversary of our church, First United Methodist Church, Tupelo, Mississippi.

(Dad spoke that day for the laity – October 24, 1999.)

:1 "O God, thou art my God, I seek thee, my soul thirsts for thee...

:2 So I have looked upon thee in the sanctuary, beholding thy power and glory."

Our church has been a vital part of my life all of my life. I was baptized there, confirmed there, escorted Kirk down the aisle there, memorialized Mama and Dad and many more relatives there, been inspired there to go out from there into the world to try to respond to the many blessings I have received.

Jack Reed, Jr.

99. <u>Psalm 67:1</u>.

"May God be gracious to us and bless us and make his face to shine upon us."

I hope that God can smile when he looks at me. (Or at least laughs!) I would love to see that.

Jack Reed, Jr.

100. Psalm 84.

:2 "My soul longs, yea faints for the courts of the Lord."

5 ways the church teaches us to go on the journey to find God:
1) to worship
2) to pray
3) to receive the sacrament of Holy Communion
4) to study the Bible
5) to serve."

Rev. Jim Curtis

101. Psalm 100.

"Make a joyful noise to the Lord, all the lands.
Serve the Lord with gladness!
Come into his presence with singing!

Know that the Lord is God!
It is he that has made us and we are his;
We are his people, and the sheep of his pasture.

Enter his gates with thanksgiving,
And his courts with praise!
Give thanks to him, bless his name!

For the Lord is good;
His steadfast love endures forever,
And his faithfulness to all generations."

102. <u>Psalm 100</u>.

An attitude of gratitude.

Authentic thanksgiving is <u>receiving</u> blessings from God, saying "Thank you" and then <u>being</u> a blessing to others.

This understanding is one of the cornerstones of my theology and my faith.

Out of gratitude, we serve others.

Jack Reed, Jr.

103. <u>Psalm 119</u>.

:105 "Thy word is a lamp to my feet and a light to my path."

"Wisdom literature instructs us how to live. 'Fundamentalists' separate faith and reason. <u>We should not do it</u>. It is not biblical. We come to know God's revelation thru the mind."

Rev. Cliff Davis

104. <u>Psalm 121</u>.

"I lift up my eyes to the hills. From whence does my help come? My help come from the Lord, who made heaven and earth.

He will not let your foot be moved,
He who keeps you will not slumber.
Behold, he who keeps Israel will neither slumber nor sleep.

The Lord is your keeper.
The Lord is your shade on your right hand,
The sun shall not smite you by day, nor the moon by night.

The Lord will keep you from all evil: he will keep your life.

The Lord will keep your going out and your coming in from this time forth and for evermore."

105. Psalm 130:5-6. (An Old Testament "Advent" Psalm)

"I wait for the Lord, my soul waits, and in his word, I hope; my soul waits for the Lord more than the watchman for the morning."

We are waiting for God at times; to guide us, to strengthen us, to love us, to forgive us, to be with us.

This was (is) Jesus-Emanuel, "God with us."

(New Testament)

106. Psalm 139. ("The Runaway Bunny" Psalm)

:7 "Whither shall I go from they Spirit? Or whither shall I flee from thy presence?

:8 If I ascend to heaven, thou art there! If I make my bed in Sheol, thou art there!

:9 If I take the wings of the morning and dwell in the uttermost parts of the sea,

:10 even there thy hand shall lead me, and thy right hand shall hold me."

This Psalm reminds me of the lovely children's book "The Runaway Bunny".

Wherever the little bunny goes, his (or her) mother says she will follow her. It is one my favorite children's books.

Jack Reed, Jr.

107. Proverbs – Summary.

- He who is open-minded can take instruction and will succeed.
- Jesus agreed with "Blessed are the humble – humility is the way to a better life."
- "The disciplined life is the way to a wholesome life."
- Values to live by produce the "narrow" way.

Rev. Cliff Davis

108. The Proverbs.

Goodness is that which <u>does</u> good. It is constructive.

<u>Evil</u> is destructive.

Goodness in Israel was social – it was the claims of the community, not private goodness.

The righteous man's life is in order.

<u>The Proverbs</u> lay out this order – what it looks like.

Wisdom led to righteousness.

Proverb 1:7 "Fear" of God should mean "obedience" to the will of God.

Rev. Cliff Davis

109. Proverbs 3:3-4.

> :3   Let not loyalty and faithfulness forsake you; bind them about your neck, write them on the tablet of your heart.

> :4   So you will find favor and good repute in the sight of God and man."

Loyalty is one of the character traits that I personally find most important in life.

Loyalty to my family, to my friends, to my church, to my work.

It also means "loyalty to the absent" – a Stephen Covey phrase. I also appreciate loyalty to me.

Jack Reed, Jr.

110. Proverbs 5:13-19

> :15   Drink water from your own cistern, flowing water from your own well.

> :16   Should your springs be scattered abroad, streams of water in the streets?

> :17   Let them be for yourself alone, and not for strangers with you.

:18   Let your fountain be blessed, <u>and rejoice in the wife of your youth</u>,

:19   a lovely hind, a graceful doe.
       Let her affection fill you at all times with delight,
       be always infatuated with her love.

Be loyal to your spouse. Period.

Jack Reed, Jr.

111. <u>The Proverbs</u>.

"We don't have to worry so much about the <u>fruits</u> of the tree if the <u>roots</u> of the tree are good." This is the point of view of the New Testament: it begins with your inside and believes the outside life will naturally come out. Whereas the Old Testament taught that if you <u>act right</u> (outside) then your inside will become right."

Rev. Cliff Davis

112. <u>The Proverbs</u>.

The way you express your love of God is by loving your neighbor.

Simply love your neighbor as yourself.

However, if you are not mature enough to live this way, then you better just follow the law.

Rev. Cliff Davis

113. The Proverbs.

Paul called Jesus "the wisdom of God."

Jesus' teachings were not only compassionate and loving, but also very wise.

Rev. Cliff Davis

114. Proverbs 10:17.

"He who heeds instruction is on the path to life, but he who rejects reproof goes astray."

Humility means you are willing to accept, to change, to learn, to become a better person.

Rev. Cliff Davis

115. Proverbs 11:14.

"Where there is no guidance, a people falls;" 'The Tupelo Spirit' is leadership which cares more about the community than the leaders care about themselves.

Rev. Cliff Davis

116. Proverbs.

"Whenever a big tree falls, it kills some little trees around it. Whenever a big man falls, it affects some little people around him."

I take this to mean that we should be mindful of the consequences of leaders' actions to those around them.

Jack Reed, Jr.

117. Proverbs 11:17.

"A man who is kind benefits himself."

Showing mercy is good for our own soul.

("Blessed are the merciful.")

Rev. Cliff Davis

118. Proverbs 11:25.

"A liberal man will be enriched."

My own father was a great example of a generous man, with his time and his money. I have tried to be generous too. It enriches your enjoyment of life; it enriches your relationships. And if you feel good about giving money, you really don't worry about not having it.

Jack Reed, Jr.

119. Proverbs 11:25.

"A liberal will be enriched."

Alternatively, an unhappy woman (man) is always checking her wallet, stingy.

120. Proverbs 12:16.

"A wise man listens to advice."

Good minds seek good minds.

Wise men listen to other wise men.

Rev. Cliff Davis

121. Proverbs 12:16.

"The vexation of a fool is known at once, but the prudent man ignores an insult."

My father was the best person I ever met at letting criticism roll off his back. Harboring anger and revenge and hate really do much more harm to oneself that to the object of the dislike.

Jack Reed, Jr.

122. Proverbs 14:34.

"Righteousness exalts a nation..."

Q. What does it mean "to love your country"?

A. The quality of our love of country is shaped by the other values that we love: The Declaration of Independence says that our forefathers began with ideas and values, and then established our government to secure them. Thus we love our nation best when we make it subservient to the highest ideals we know.

We must live above the standards around us, and thus raise those standards.

We must begin with ourselves.

Still we must celebrate what is right about our nation.

Rev. Jim McCormack

123. <u>Proverbs 15:1,4.</u>

> :1 "A soft answer turns away wrath, but a harsh word stirs up anger.

> :4 "A gentle tongue is a tree of life, but perverseness in it breaks the spirit."

"You can break the spirit of a friend, or a husband or a wife, with a harsh word."

Rev. Cliff Davis

124. <u>Proverbs 18:8.</u>

> :8 "... he who keeps understanding will prosper."

"The biggest blunders I have made in my life have been in situations where I did not understand."

Rev. Cliff Davis

125. <u>Proverbs 18:14.</u>

> :14 "A man's spirit will endure sickness; but a broken spirit who can bear?"

If a man (or woman) has a strong will, he (or she) can endure; if not, anything can get him (or her) down

Rev. Cliff Davis

126. <u>Proverbs 22:1.</u>

> :1 "A good name is to be chosen rather than great riches."

It is a privilege to be handed a good name, and it is a responsibility to pass one down.

127. Proverbs 31:10-31.

:10 "A good wife who can find? She is far more precious than jewels.

:11- The heart of her husband trusts in her...

:20 She opens her hand to the poor, and reaches out her hand to the needy...

:25 Strength and dignity are her clothing, and she laughs at the time to come.

:26 She opens her mouth with wisdom, and the teaching of kindness is on her tongue.

:27 She looks well to the ways of her household and does not eat the bread of idleness.

:28 Her children rise up and call her blessed; her husband also, and he praises her.

:29 "Many women have done excellently, but you surpass then all..."

Dad, David, Tate, Jack, and I all found one!

Jack Reed, Jr.

128. Proverbs.

"We instantly know certain truths: what is right, what is wrong, help vs harm, love vs hate, truth vs lies. We know these things because we have in us a spark of divinity."

Rev. Cliff Davis

129. <u>Ecclesiastes.</u>

Faced with despair you can
>> Give up.
>> Blow up,
>> Or grow up.

130. <u>Ecclesiastes 3:1-9.</u>

"For everything there is a season, and a time for everything under heaven:
A time to be born, and a time to die;
A time to plant, and a time to pluck what is planted;
A time to kill, and a time to heal;
A time to break down, and a time to build up;
A time to weep, and a time to laugh;
A time to mourn, and a time to dance;
A time to cast away stones, and a time to gather stones together;
A time to embrace, and a time to refrain from embracing;
A time to seek, and a time to lose;
A time to keep, and a time to cast away;
A time to rend, and a time to sew;
A time to keep silence, and a time to speak;
A time love, and a time to hate;
A time for war, and a time for peace."

131. We love God by loving people.

132. You character is your destiny.

    Your principles determine you actions and reactions.

133. <u>Ecclesiastes.</u>

    Regarding patience:

    Our forefathers used to wait two weeks for a stagecoach.

    We almost have a cardiac arrest if we miss the first panel of a revolving door.

134. We all stand on someone else's shoulders:

    God gave us life;
    Our parents give us love;
    Our soldiers, freedom;
    Our teacher, knowledge.
       Have the humility to recognize and appreciate them.

135. There are things in the world that God wants done – and they won't get done.

    If we don't do it.
    We can bring love.
    We can bring caring, without being heroic or famous.
    But we are being noble.

136. God's grace is not only meant to be <u>enjoyed</u>, but to be <u>employed</u>.

137. "The First Song of Isaiah".

> Surely it is God who saves me;
> I will trust in him and not be afraid
> For the Lord is my stronghold and my sure defence, and
> he will be my Savior.

138. Isaiah 12:2.

> "Behold God is my salvation,
> I will trust, and will not be afraid;
> For the Lord God is my strength and my song,
> And he has become my salvation."

This verse has inspired one of my favorite songs:

> "Surely it is God who saves me
> I will trust in him and not be afraid;
> For the Lord is my stronghold and my sure defence,
> And he will be my savior."

(Also the anthem: "He's Never Failed Me, ... yet."
(P. 2020 Hymnal)

139. Isaiah 40:3-5.

> :3   "A voice cries:
> "In the wilderness prepare the way of the Lord,
> make straight in the desert a highway for our God.

> :4   Every valley shall be lifted up, and every mountain
> and hill made low; the uneven ground shall
> become level, and the rough places a plain.

:5   And the glory of the Lord shall be revealed, and all flesh shall see it together; for the mouth of the Lord has spoken (it)."

Isaiah was preparing the Jews for their deliverance.

Christians read into this passage God's deliverance of <u>all</u> His people.

140. <u>Isaiah 35.</u>

:5   "Then the eyes of the blind shall be opened; ... the thirsty ground springs of water ... the grass shall become reeds and rushes."

(☺Nice that John Rush and his family and our family were together in biblical times!)

141. <u>Isaiah 40:30-31.</u>

:30   "Even youths shall faint and be weary, and young men fall exhausted;

:31   but they who wait for the Lord shall renew their strengths, they shall mount up with wings like eagles, they shall run and not be weary, they shall walk and not faint."

Inspirational metaphor.

142. <u>Isaiah 42:3.</u>

"A bruised reed I will not break."

☺ A happy assurance! (for our family!)

143. Lamentations 3:22-23.

> :22 "The steadfast love of the Lord never ceases, his mercies never come to an end;
>
> :23 they are new every morning."

I say my prayers in the morning to help guide my day.

Annie – "The sun will come out tomorrow."

We must always have hope.

144. Ezekiel 37:7,10.

> :7 "... and as I prophesied, there was a noise, and behold a rattling; and the bones came together bone to bone.
>
> :10 So I prophesied as he commanded me, and the breath came into them, and they lived, and stood upon their feet ..."

All of our bones are white, no matter what skin color surrounds them.

God put breath into every one of us.

His spirit brings us life.

His spirit can make something happen.

145. "Regarding the nature miracles, I'm an agnostic. I just don't know.

Like Leslie Weatherhead, "I have put them in a drawer labeled 'awaiting further light.'"

Rev. Cliff Davis

146. <u>Amos 5:24</u>.

"But let justice roll down like waters, and righteousness like an ever-flowing stream."

(Amos was the 1st Book of the Bible to be written down.)

This line was part of Dr. Martin Luther King, Jr.'s "I Have A Dream" speech on the Mall in front of the Lincoln Memorial.

147. The Book of Jonah – Thoughts.

The Book of Jonah is a short story intended to teach a lesson: that God can redeem us in unexpected moments, in unexpected places, in unexpected voices.

"The word of God is in the Bible, but not every word in the Bible is the word of God."

It is not to be taken literally.

Rev. Cliff Davis

148. <u>Zechariah 4:6</u>.

"Not by might nor by power, but by my spirit says the Lord of hosts."

(By God, we can too!)

149. <u>Micah 6:8.</u> One of the greatest verses in the Bible.

"He has showed you, O man, what is good; and what does the Lord require of you but to do justice, and to love kindness, and to walk humbly with your God?"

In this simple sentence the prophet sums up the legal, ethical, and spiritual requirements of religion.

150. One interpretation of the phrase "have faith in Jesus" is "have the faith of Jesus."

Richard Rohr

I like this idea. It seems to be a guide for us as we try to be "followers of the Way".

151. Jesus' time in history:

The Romans provided the highways for transportation and communication. The Greeks provided the universal language.

The Jews had provided the dream of light into darkness, of a Messiah.

So when Jesus came "the Word was made flesh".

152. I like to remember that the word "holy" and "whole" come from the same root. That means that to be holy is to have all of life made whole, made whole because all the varied parts of life are gathered and organized around their proper center. And for Christians, that proper center is God made known in Jesus.

Rev. Jim McCormick

153. Christianity does not explain away the chaos of life.

Instead our faith calls us to follow Jesus and to believe that the perplexing contradictions of life need not defeat us.

154. The New Testament.

The New Testament comprises 27 books.
A more appropriate word than "testament" to designate the character of these books is "covenant"; the relationship that God established with his people.
The books were written within a period of somewhat less than 100 years. Four of them are "Gospels" because they tell the "gospel" (a word derived from the Anglo-Saxon god-spell, meaning "good tidings" of Jesus Christ. His birth, baptism, ministry of teaching and healing, death, and resurrection.)

155. The Mission Statement of First United Methodist Church, Tupelo, Mississippi:

"Love God, Love Neighbor. Celebrate and serve Christ together."

Jack Reed, Jr.

156. Prayer.

Does the first violinist tune the orchestra after the performance? No. He tunes it before the performance. This reasoning was why I switched my regular prayer time to the early mornings. It helps me to remember how and what I want to be and do each day. (I still like bedtime prayers too, though.)

Jack Reed, Jr.

157. <u>Worship</u>. (per Jim McCormick)

The congregation, the pastor, the choir – are all the stage. God is the audience.

The laity come to celebrate what God has done for us in Christ.

158. (4 Day Combination)   (per Cliff Davis)

Day 1: 3 Principles for Life (A Life Worth Living)

1) You've got to have something good and constructive to do.
2) You've got to find someone to love.
3) You've got to find something to believe in.

Day 2: Principle 1: You've got to have something good and constructive to do.
- "Jesus went about doing good.
- Volunteer at Helping Hands, non-profit jobs.
- Paul, in prison, wrote letters.
- Work at your job.

Day 3: Principle 2: You've got to find someone to love.

- Most have family. ("Most divorces could be prevented if we treated our family as well as we treat our friends." – marriage counselor.)

45

- If not family, friends.
- If not friends, pets.
- And there are others who need love. (The Good Samaritan found a stranger along the roadside.)

Day 4: Principle 3: You've got to find something to believe in.
- Something to trust in.
- Something to place your hope upon.

159. We honor those who need our help by treating them as equals, understanding that we are all God's children. I often think, if this woman were my daughter, I would hope someone would help her.- Jack Reed, Jr.

160. Our destiny is our <u>character</u>.

Jesus could not be true to himself and escape the cross.

The cross was freedom and destiny.

Jack Reed, Jr.

161. At our best we need to have a place in our philosophy – in our theology – that will help us during the storms of our lives; we <u>will</u> have troubles. Nature is indifferent to us. The Providence of God doesn't mean no pain, but ultimately God is for good. This is the basic meaning of the resurrection.

Rev. Cliff Davis

162. Lean into the future.

163. I believe we are summoned by God to see in the human other a trace of the divine Other.

Rabbi Jonathan Sacks

164. The gospel is more of a witness than an explanation.

165. A personal thought on 6-1-14.

"Listening to the choir sing, I am struck again, as I am every Sunday, by how beautiful Lisa is, how much I love her, and how proud I am of her loyal service in our choir for 38 years."

166. Matthew: Is writing 70 years or so after Jesus has gone. He is preaching using the spirit of Jesus, and his teachings. "Don't worry about the literal words – get to the point. Emphasize the things that are <u>important</u> – the things that we can build life upon.

"Paul Tillach: 2 things are indisputable:
1) Jesus lived and people were magnetized by the kind of person he was.
2) Jesus was (is) the Christ."

Rev. Cliff Davis

167. <u>Matthew 1:25</u>.

"and he called his name Jesus."

Jesus means "God saves"; or "he will save".

"It is what Jesus does: he saves the woman at the well; he saves the tax collector; he can do that with us too."

Rev. Jim Curtis

168. Christmas.

The best way to send an idea is to wrap it up in person. God expressed himself in human form in the person of Jesus.

Emmanuel – "God is with us."

169. Matthew 2: The Christmas Story with the Wise Men.

Christmas is a love story: the story of Joseph's love for Mary and hers for him; of God's love for the world. But once we find Jesus and fall down and worship him, we are to get up and follow him – in love, in service, in self-giving. Our own journey is then with Jesus, and we will have abundant life.

Rev. Jim McCormick

170. Matthew 2: The Birth of Jesus.

Rev. Jim McCormick told a story of an American soldier who was visiting an orphanage overseas. He asked one little boy what he would like for Christmas and the boy answered, "Just hold me." The soldier did, "and it was Christmas".

Imagine God reaching down and holding the world – hugging us, just as Joseph held the baby Jesus.

This is the Christmas story.

171. Matthew 1: The birth of Jesus.

Regarding the virgin birth:

1:22 "Behold a virgin shall conceive and bear a son, and his name shall be called Emanuel (which means God is with us)."

"Regardless of the mystery of the immaculate conception, the Holy Spirit was present at Jesus' birth."

Rev. Cliff Davis

172. Matthew 3: John the Baptist.

"There is no sadder commentary that that the Light tried to come into the world but people preferred darkness."

Rev. Larry Goodpastor

173. Matthew 4: Jesus' baptism.

Our baptism:

1) Connects us with God.

2) Calls us to be children of God.

Rev. Jim McCormick

(JR – I don't believe that little children are "sinners" until baptized.)

174. Matthew 5: The Beatitudes.

The Beatitudes are not laws; they are the spirit of Christ.

They are characteristics of life in the Kingdom of God right here on earth.

They teach us how to live in God's grace.

Rev. Cliff Davis

175. Matthew 5:5: The 3rd Beatitude.

5:5 "Blessed are the meek for they shall inherit the earth."

"Meekness" does not equal

"weakness." Understand this as "self-control."

176. Matthew 5:14. "You are the light of the world."

- "Light is positive; it plows the darkness under."

Robert Lewis Stevenson

- In London when the streets were lit with oil lamps a father asked his young son, who was staring out his window, "what are you looking at?" The boy answered, "I'm watching a man make holes in the darkness."
Jesus "Let you light so shine before men, that they may see your good works, and give glory to your Father in Heaven."

- The image of our sanctuary at the Christmas Eve Candlelight Service.

Jack Reed, Jr.

177. Matthew 5:14: "You are the light of the world."

Light is comforting.
Light guides us.
We share the light by the kind of person we are.

We can illumine the world we share with others.

178. <u>Matthew 5:42</u>: "Give to him who begs from you, and do not refuse him who would borrow from you."

JR – I have often loaned money to those who have asked me, and rarely have I been repaid. Yet I don't regret doing it because I have always felt so fortunate in my life.

(That doesn't mean that I give cash to alcoholics or drug addicts.)

I give it almost always <u>without</u> asking that it be repaid. This is a personal ministry/charity I have named "BALM".

179. Theology by Rev. Cliff Davis

"I don't take one line out of Jesus' teachings and say, 'This is absolutely what Jesus meant'. I take the entire sweep of the Christian revelation and think of how it fits into the concept of a life of love."

[It takes it all (not just a line or two) to build a real theology.]

"Jesus came to reveal the love of God." C.D.

180. Prayer.

Prayer doesn't change God, it changes us.

The gift of prayer is intimacy with God; communion with God.

181. Matthew 6:19.

     "Do not lay up for yourselves treasures on earth ... but lay up for yourselves treasures in heaven ... For where your treasure is there your heart be also."

     This verse was the one Lisa and I used when I was asked to lead the church stewardship campaign at age 29.

     It is also the verse that inspired Henry van Dyke to write The Mansion – one of my favorite stories.

182. Matthew 8:5.

     "And he stretched out his hand and touched him ..."

     Touching can express love. It has power.

     It has meaning.

     A warm handshake. A hug.

183. Prayer – per Grandpa in Cold Sassy Tree, a novel by Olive Ann Burns:
     "Non-praying folks and praying folks seem to have about the same things happen to them in life – make about as much money, get sick, die; the best thing about prayer is to be able to sit down and visit with God like an old friend; instead of going into a storekeeper and trying to talk to him into a bargain."

     Per Rev. Bill McAlilly

184. St. Augustine.

In essential things, unity; in non-essential things, freedom; in <u>all</u> things, charity.

185. Remember our life itself is a gift; we did nothing to get it, to deserve it.

When grace comes into your life, you see every other person as a thing of value.

Rev. Cliff Davis

186. Even more than wanting our wounds healed, we want our hurts acknowledged, known.

"People really don't mind if you disagree, they just want to be heard."

Chancellor Robert Khayat

187. Jesus gives us the vision and accompanies us on the journey.

188. We need to find the time to mediate; time to pray; time to worship.

Despite our busy lives we need to find time for quiet reflection.

189. As you grow older, (per Cliff Davis):

1) Take care of your body. Keep active. Exercise. Eat smart. Go to the doctor for a physical. Do physical work.

2) Nourish your mind. Use it. Always be a reader. A thinker. A writer.

3) Cultivate your spirit. Meditate. Worship. Spiritual listening, reading, thinking.

(Boy Scout Motto: "Physically strong. Mentally awake. Morally strong.")

190. Matthew 8:23-27. Jesus calming the storm.

More important than believing in the nature miracles is the belief that Jesus can still the storms of the heart, of the spirit, of anxiety, of hatred, of fear, of grief.

Rev. Cliff Davis

191. Jesus was a religious genius.

He had a capacity – a unique capacity – to receive the spirit of God.

192. Attending church.

We need to come to church every Sunday to be restored, to recharge our batteries; to be reminded of the grace and mercy of God; to center ourselves in a pathway of love.

I <u>always</u> am glad I've gone to church – to see an old friend or introduce a new friend – or be reminded to get in touch with someone who has had a tough time, or a good time in their life.

193. Matthew 9:36.

"When he saw the crowds, he had <u>compassion</u> for them ..."

Compassion = "to care with passion".

194. Matthew 10:39.

"He who finds his life will lose it, and he who loses his life for my sake will find it."

Find a cause bigger than yourself; then lose yourself in it.

Jesus saw our world transformed thru ordinary people.

195. Regarding others' beliefs:

We should be tolerant of others, but we cannot please everybody, and we should not let ourselves be victims of what others believe.

Be true to ourselves. Be willing to grow.

Try to always criticize the principle with which we disagree, and not the person,

196. Regarding doubt:

Sincere doubt can be a spur to a more intelligent faith.

Paul Tillach said that doubt was a part of faith.

197. There is no act of ministry too small.

198. Matthew 11:20-24.

…You shall be brought down in Sodom…

Rev. Cliff Davis: "I don't believe Jesus actually said these verses. I believe that they were added by the early church."

JR. (Just as Jesus ignored legislative laws such as not healing on the Sabbath, Cliff Davis ignores part of the New Testament which he feels are not consistent with the real message of Jesus.)

199. Matthew 12:33.

"… for the tree is known by its fruit …"

Our behavior – our lives – speak to our values – not our words about our values.

200. If we are too busy to pray and to busy to nurture our souls, we are too busy.

201. Judgment.

Socrates: "He who takes only a few things into account, finds it easy to pass judgment."

We humans make mistakes. So when we think of forgiveness, remember forgiveness is for us as well as from us. Mercy, grace.

Be aware of the full breadth of our lives.

202. Forgiveness:

On the cross Jesus asks God to forgive his persecutors. And when Jesus arose from the dead, he didn't assemble a posse and get revenge on them.

203. Faith:

The opposite of faith is fear. People without faith fear there is never enough.

Faith is trust, and faith is the willingness to live our lives as Jesus instructed us.

204. Violence in America:

To have less violence in America we need to train less violent people.

All of us have desires for pleasure and to avoid pain. But what shall we do about these desires?

We look at desires through the mind and direct them through the <u>will</u>.

Per Sigmund Freud: "Put a lid on the id."

Rev. Cliff Davis

205. There is much evidence on several levels that there are at least two major tasks to human life. the first task is to build a strong "container" or identity; the second is to find the contents that the container was meant to hold.

Richard Rohr

206. Busy lives:

If we are too busy to play and to nourish our soul, we are too busy.

207. Forgiveness:

Forgiveness is not the same thing as weakness. It is strength and power and love.

Rev. Prentiss Gordon

208. <u>Matthew 13:45-46</u>.

> :45 "The Kingdom of heaven is like a merchant in search of fine pearls,
>
> :46 who on finding one pearl of great value, went and sold all he had and bought it."

Spiritual treasures money <u>cannot</u> buy: hope, love, charity, compassion are worth than more money.

(Q. What is the most valuable "find" I've had? Lisa!)

209. <u>Matthew 14:13-21</u>. Feed the five thousand with 5 loaves and 2 fish.

The disciples underestimated Jesus and their own resources.

"So much need, so little resources." If we are not careful we can be overwhelmed by the enormity of the tasks.

We are not asked to give more than we can give – nor are we asked to give less.

210. <u>Matthew 14</u>.

Jesus had a healthy rhythm to his life.

Prayer ⇨ service to others ⇨ time with friends ⇨ prayer.

211. Jesus – "The Inviter:

Kierkeguard

My personal mission statement:

"Jesus wants life to be a party; it's just up to us to make sure that everyone is invited."

Jack Reed, Jr.

212. <u>Matthew 16:18-19</u>.

:18　"And I tell you, you are Peter, and on this rock I will build my church, and and the powers of death shall not prevail against it.

:19　I will give you the keys to the Kingdom of heaven..."

God has made us (like he did with Peter) responsible partners in the success of the Christian enterprise.

We have been given authority and responsibility.

We hold the keys.

We make possible good things as a result of our effective stewardship.

We can either open doors, leave them closed, or close them.

"I couldn't get excited about a Christ who only asked for our leftovers."

Rev. Jim McCormick

213. Matthew 16:18. The Church.

"... you are Peter, and on this rock I will build my church."

The church is people.

Christ himself said "I will build my church" on a person, Peter.

It has been passed on from generation to generation by the grace of God, touching people who touch other people, who find grace.

When the church has been faithful to its Lord it has been the best institution in this world: building schools, hospitals, orphanages.

It has profoundly affected my own life: thanks to my parents, Lisa and children, pastors, fellow church members and family.

The church is at work today: people know each other by name. We find affirmation, a cheering section. We renew our vision, our inspiration.

214. <u>Matthew 16:24-26</u>.

:24 "Then Jews told his disciples, "If any man would come after me, let him deny himself and <u>take up his cross</u> and follow me.

:25 For whoever would save his life will lose it, and whoever loses his life for my sake will find it.

:26 For what would it profit a man, if he gains the whole world and forfeits his life? Or what shall a man give in return for his life?"

To pick up the cross, we may have to put some other things down.

215. <u>Matthew 16:24</u>. (also Mark 8:34)

"If a man would come after me, let his deny himself and <u>take up his cross and follow me.</u>

"Jesus didn't say what the cross looks like; he didn't say for how far; he didn't say for how long."

John Fling
Columbia, South Carolina

(I heard John Fling on Charles Kuralt's Christmas tape and was so impressed and inspired by his example that I insisted Kirk and Jack and Lisa hear his story. I also called and spoke with him and made a contribution to his ministry.)

216. Christian discipleship is not church membership.

217. Jesus didn't say, "Follow me to church."

He said, "follow me ... to heal, to love, to help, to sacrifice, to live a life of service."

To live a life of passion, without pretense, with purpose.

218. "I look for the spiritual significance of Jesus' teachings, not seeing Jesus as a new lawgiver.

So it is not essential to obey each passage literally."

Rev. Cliff Davis

219. ☺
"The only way you can love some people is to love them and leave them alone."

Rev. Cliff Davis

220. Nothing, finally, can separate us from the love of God.

Jesus' cross falls like a bridge between us and God.

God ↔ us

221. We cannot separate our relationship with God from our relationships with others

(i.e. "Forgive us our trespasses as we forgive others.")

Rev. Jim McCormick

222. Matthew 20:26.

"whoever would be great among you must be your servant."

Jesus defined "Messiahship" from King to servant, from might to the power of suffering.

223. Matthew 22:36-40.

:36 "Teacher, which is the great commandment in the law?

:37 And he said to him, "You shall love the Lord your God with all your heart, and with all your soul, and with all your mind.

:38 This is the great and first commandment.

:39 And a second is like it. You shall love your neighbor as yourself.

:40 On these two commandments depend all the law and the prophets."

Here Jesus goes beyond legalism, literalism, and spoke to the spirit of the law. Jesus insisted that our relationship with God is central. That overflows into our relationships with others.

Rev. Jim McCormick

224. Matthew 25:31-40.

"... :34 Then the King will say to those of his right hand, "Come, O blessed of my father, inherit the Kingdom prepared for you from the foundation of the world.

:35 For I was hungry and you gave me food, I was thirsty and you gave me drink, I was a stranger and you welcomed me,

:36 I was naked and you clothed me, I was sick and you visited me, I was in prison and you came to me.

:37 Then the righteous will answer him, "Lord when did we see thee hungry and feed thee, or thirsty and give thee drink?

:38 And when did we see thee a stranger and welcome thee or naked and clothe thee?

:39 And when did we see thee sick or in prison and visit thee?"

:40 And the King will answer them, "Truly, I say to you, as you did it to one of the least of these my brethren, you did it unto me."

225. <u>Matthew 25:31-40</u>. "When you did it to one of the least of these ... you did it unto me."

Whenever we turn our backs on people, we turn our backs on Jesus; whoever they are, whatever their needs.

The greatest commandment: "Love God, love neighbors."

No matter how important our spiritual lives, or holiness, the gospel also requires a mission dimension. And how we live our mission life indicates our spiritual heart.

226. Matthew 26:36-37, 39.

Jesus, following the Last Supper, went to Gethsemane and took his closest friends, Peter, James, and John.

Jesus didn't hide his feelings from his friends.

(Who would I take?)

But his best decision was to pray.

:39 "My Father, if it be possible, let this cup pass from me; nevertheless, not as I will but as thou wilt."

227. Jesus proactively went to Jerusalem. Palm Sunday

He could have said that "discretion is the better part of valor" and not gone.

But he chose to go.

So perhaps the real "triumphant entry" on Palm Sunday was the triumph of Jesus' personal integrity and obedience to God.

228. Matthew 27:22

"Pilate said to them, 'Then what shall I do with Jesus who is called Christ?'"

What shall I do with Jesus?

1. Ignore him?
2. Reject him?
3. Follow him?

229. Easter – Good Friday.

"There is no comfort in Good Friday, only mourning. We must wait for Easter morning and joy.

Weep, grieve ... then rise up."

Carlyle Marney per Cliff Davis

230. Easter Morning – Matthew 28.

Easter morning: it is not the news someone broke into the tomb, but that Jesus broke out of the tomb.

Rev. Jim Curtis

Jesus didn't escape death, he conquered it.

Rev. Jim Curtis

231. Matthew 28:20.

Jesus: "... and lo, I am with you always, to the close of the age."

Jesus is saying "I am blessing your life. Follow your dream."

232. "Everywhere you go preach; and if necessary, use words."

St. Francis of Assisi

233. The evidence of our Christian faith will be seen in our deeds.

We reveal in our witness what we believe.

234. <u>Mark 1:9-11</u>.

When Jesus was baptised he found that he was not tapped for fame and recognition, but for service.

Our baptism launches us on our own life's journey as one of God's people.

235. <u>Mark 1:11</u>.

"Thou art my beloved Son with <u>whom I am well pleased</u>."

For Jesus this was an <u>affirmation</u> from his father of his life – of his work. Every son needs this. Every daughter.

It is psychologically central.

236. <u>Mark 1:17</u>.

:17 "And Jesus said to (Simon and Andrew), 'Follow me and I will make you fishers of men."

To follow Jesus means to care for other people.

237. <u>Mark 1:40-42</u>. Jesus healing a leper.

:41 "Moved with pity he stretched his hand and touched him."

Read this story and substitute "ourselves" for "Jesus".

If we have the will and the compassion, we can help others best.

"The church is the church only when it serves others."

Deidrich Bonnhoffer

We are called to extend the touch of Jesus – we extend God's grace.

238. Mark 2:5. Jesus healing the paralytic.

"… my son your sins are forgiven."

"True forgiveness is a miracle."

Rev. Jim Curtis

239. Mark 4:1-20. The parable of the sower of the seeds.

This is the first parable of the first book of the New Testament.

God is the sower. Sowing God's grace.

Let us be receptive.

Jesus challenges us to be "the good soil".

240. Mark 4:35-41. The story of Jesus calming the storm at sea.

Most of the time life's storms come when we least expect them.

Most come with one word: "cancer", "diabetes", "fire", "accident".

Jesus can still the storms of our lives.

This story is filled with symbolism. Jesus shows no fear, no anxiety Just courage and faith.

Jesus calms our hearts.

Jesus is in the boat with us.

241. <u>Mark 2:15-16</u>. Jesus sitting with tax collectors and sinners.

> :15 And as he sat at table in his house, many tax collectors and sinners were sitting with·Jesus and his disciples; for there were many who followed him.

> :16 And the scribes of the Pharisees, when they saw that he was eating with sinners and tax collectors, said to his disciples, "Why does he eat with tax collectors and sinners?"

Jesus could separate the sin from the sinner.

Jesus built bridges.

"Jesus never lost his taste for bad company."

Rev. Jim McCormick

242. <u>Mark 4:21</u>. Is a lamp ... under a bushel ... (or) on a stand?

Brother Bo Holloman loved people.

His lamp was on a lampstand.

Rev. Cliff Davis

243. <u>Mark 2:1-11, 17</u>. Jesus healing the paralytic carried to Jesus by four friends.

:2   "And many were gathered together, so that there was no room for them, not even about the door; and he was preaching the word to them.

:3   And they came, bringing to him a paralytic carried by four men.

:4   And when they could not get near him because of the crowd, they removed the roof above him; and when they made an opening, they let down on which the paralytic lay.

:5   And when Jesus saw their faith, he said to the paralytic, "My son your sins are forgiven...

:17   Rise, take up your pallet and go home."

The four friends are the real heroes of the story. Their faith is marked by creativity and compassion, ingenuity, and persistence.

Rev. Larry Goodpastor

PS. (DWIT – Do Whatever It Takes)

244. Mark 2:1-12. Jesus healing a paralytic carried to Jesus by four friends.

Pray for good friends.
Pray to be a good friend.
When we are paralyzed, we need friends to pick us up.
We need to be a friend.
We are called to the ministry of Christian friendship.

Rev. Chris McAllily

245. A good ritual leads to a good life.

Rev. Cliff Davis

246. Mark 6:13. "And they (the disciples) cast out many demons, and anointed with oil many that were sick and healed them."

The disciples' lives were aligned with Jesus' life.

If our lives are aligned with Jesus' (God's) will we become vessels of his power; like an ordinary drinking straw that, when aligned just right, permits the power of the Mississippi River to flow through it.

Rev. Andy Ray

247. Mark 6:31. "And (Jesus) said to (the disciples), 'Come away by yourselves to a lonely place and rest for a while.'

We need to find our own quiet, still place.

God is our refuge and strength; let Him be.

248. Mark 6:34: Jesus teaching the throng.

:34 "As he landed, he saw a great throng, and he had compassion on them, because they were like sheep without a shepherd; and he began to teach them many things."

A great verse to inspire our teachers.

Teaching is critical to our civilization.

249. Mark 6:37. "You (the disciples) give them something to eat."

Jesus is telling us, today, "You give them something to eat."

250. Our creeds are less important than our deeds.

251. Mark 8:34.

"If a man would come after me, let him deny himself and take up his cross and follow me."

He didn't say what the cross would look like; he didn't say for how far or for how long to carry it.

John Fling (see also note on Matthew 16:24)

252. Mark 8:34, 36-37.

:34 "If any man would come after me, let him deny himself and take up his cross and follow me ...

:36 For what does it profit a man to gain the whole world and forfeit his life?

:37 For what can a man give in return for his life?"

The cross is not something we must bear or endure, but something we affirmatively take up and carry.

Rev. Andy Ray

253. Mark 9:2-8. Jesus' transfiguration on the mountain top.

Jesus was not content to stay on the mountain top, but to go back down to the streets.

So, too, are we to go to the streets with him.

Rev. Jim Curtis

254. <u>Mark 9:2-8</u>. Jesus' transformation on the mountain top.

We are saved to serve.

We are to be inspired by the mountaintop, but you can't rest there.

Rev. Prentiss Gordon

255. <u>Mark 9:35</u>.

"If anyone would be first, he must be last of all – and servant of all."

Mark is giving his understanding of what it means to be a disciple of Jesus.

256. <u>Mark 9:36-37</u>.

:36 "And he took a child, and put him in the midst of them; and taking him in his arms he said to them,

:37 'Whoever receives one such child in my name receives me; and whoever receives me, receives not me but him <u>who sent me</u>.

A wonderful scene to imagine, Jesus holding a little child in his arms.

We need to hug all children.

Jack Reed, Jr.

257. <u>Mark 9:37-38</u>. The story of James and John asking to sit at (Jesus') <u>right</u> <u>hand</u> and <u>at his left</u>, in your glory."

- To be granted, don't look up; look down.
- We will drink from the cup Jesus drank from one sip at a time, day by day. We invest our lives one check at a time: one person at a time.
- Sitting with a person in a time of crisis is a sip from that cup. Teaching Sunday School is a sip. Working with MYF is a gulp!
- Every word of encouragement is a sip
- This is the <u>character</u> of a person drinking of the cup of Christ.

Rev. Jim Curtis
("Excellent!" JR)

258. <u>Mark 9:38</u>.

"John said to him, 'Teacher'."

Mark always <u>called</u> Jesus "Teacher".

To me this is one of the most important roles Jesus serves for my life.

JR

259. <u>Mark 10:8</u>. (On marriage). "What therefore God has joined <u>together</u>, let <u>not man</u> put asunder."

Only <u>commitment</u> is more important to a good marriage than <u>communication</u>.

Every family has problems and problems do not go away because we don't talk about them.

260. <u>Marriage</u>: Like an important muscle, <u>love</u> needs to be used to grow.

<u>6 Ways</u>:

1) When a problem arises, talk about it now. (Treat them like garbage and deal with them that day. Don't let it rot.)
2) <u>Listen attentively</u>.
3) Have the strength to be fallible. Humility and strength go together. Say "I'm sorry."
4) Remember in good communicating <u>winning is not the goal</u>. Understanding and getting to a win/win is.
5) Sometimes a hug beats any words.
6) Don't assume that you know what your partner wants.

Rev. Jim McCormick

261. <u>Marriage</u>.

The joy in marriage should be in the journey together.

262. <u>Mark 10:45</u>. "For the Son of Man came not to be served, but to serve."

Jesus, through his actions and his words, had been teaching that the abundant life was one full of love and service; that God loved thieves and prostitutes as much as priests. Jesus' preaching was radical then – and still is today.

263. <u>Mark 10:47</u>. "… Jesus … have mercy on me!"

Mercy is giving people what they need, not what they deserve.

(In "Les Misérables" Jean Valjean is merciful. Inspector Javert is justice personified.)

There are times when we all need mercy. There are times when we have the opportunity to be merciful to others.

264. Very often Jesus calls us to do very humble things. (As he washed the feet of his disciples.)

Also, playing a small part graciously <u>is</u> greatness.

Eg. Andrew brought his brother Peter to Jesus. While Peter became "great" – the 'rock' upon which the church was established, he might never have gotten there had not Andrew done his part.

265. As Jesus himself preached and taught and demonstrated the Kingdom of God here on earth;

the sovereignty of service,
the greatness of love,
the power of humility,
he was not alone –
God was with him – as he is today with us.

266. <u>Ministry</u> is simply doing the work of God in the arena in which we are, every day.

(Who is my neighbor?" Anyone who needs our help.)

Then God's will "will be done on earth as it is in heaven."

267. The Afterlife:

"There are 2 Biblical theories of the Afterlife.

1) I choose to believe in universal salvation.

2) Eternal hell or heaven – the only reason for this theory would be revenge and an angry God is beneath God's dignity.

"Heaven will only be heaven as it empties hell."

Rev. Cliff Davis

268. The Providence of God.

"God created the world from chaos.

Evil comes from chaos.

"Being" is coming from God.

"Non-being" is coming from chaos.

Our faith in God becomes our hope.

"The providence of God" does not abolish luck, accidents, free will, nor chance.

But God will never be ultimately defeated."

Rev. Cliff Davis

269. Good will prevail in the end.

If things are not good right now, then it's not the end.

270. <u>Mark 12:41-44</u>. Story of the widow contributing out of her poverty.

We <u>offer</u> our gratitude and our help.
These are "<u>offering</u> plates", not "collection plates".

271. <u>Mark 13</u>. Apocalyptic predictions attributed to Jesus

"Most reputable Biblical scholars believe that Jesus did not say these words. It is Mark preaching to the early church, giving early Christians directions."

Rev. Cliff Davis

272. Jesus' Second Coming.

"I am not concerned about a second coming. Ultimately Good will conquer Evil."

Rev. Cliff Davis

273. <u>Mark 14:3-9</u>. "... a woman came with an alabaster jar of ointment of pure nard, very costly, and she broke the jar and poured it over his head, ..."

:6   "Let her alone; why do you trouble her? She has done a beautiful thing to me. For you always have the poor with you, and whenever you will, you can do good to <u>them</u>; but you <u>will not always</u> have me"

This woman <u>extravagantly</u> expressed her love, her act of love, appreciation, and devotion.

Rev. John Sudduth

We need to act extravagantly towards those we love and to those who could use an extravagance.

JR

274. "It is not important how much we accomplish, but how much we love."

Mother Teresa

275. <u>Mark 14:10</u>. "Then Judas Iscariot, who was one of the twelve, went to the chief priests in order to <u>betray him to them</u>."

Rather than examine Judas' betrayal, consider how we betray Jesus from time to time. Yet God's grace is always with us. We must ask God's divine power to flow thru our human weakness, and thus go give us the strength to follow Him.

Rev. Larry Goodpastor

276. <u>Mark 14:32-36.</u> "... :36 Abba, Father, all things are possible to thee; remove this cup from me; yet <u>not what I will but what thou wilt</u>."

Jesus was expressing his desire to live honestly, yet he got silence.

Even for Jesus God did not remove "this cup of woe".

Our response to our own challenges is up to us.

277. <u>Mark 16</u>. The Risen Christ.

Our Methodist symbols of the cross and the flame are together important; for we are to be on fire for God.

278. <u>Mark 16</u>. The First Easter Morning.

:6 "Do not be amazed; you seek Jesus of Nazareth, who was crucified. He has risen, he is not here ...

:7 But go and tell his disciples and Peter that he is going before you ...

Perhaps they were to tell Peter specifically because the last time that Christ saw Peter was when Peter had denied him three times.

Forgiveness.

279. <u>Destiny</u>.

Our freedom does not avoid destiny.

Destiny are those things that come upon us without our choosing them – then we deal with them.

Rev. Cliff Davis

280. <u>Luke 1:46-56</u>. "The Magnificat" –
"My soul <u>magnifies</u> <u>the</u> <u>Lord</u> ...

The revolution of the "Magnificat":
1) The Moral: vs the Proud.
2) The Social: vs the Rich and Powerful; <u>for</u> children and the poor.
3) The Economic: vs the Haves

281. <u>Luke 2:1-20</u>

:1 And it came to pass in those days, that a decree from Caesar Augustus that all the world should be taxed.

:2 This taxing was first made when Cyrenius was governor of Syria.

:3 And all went to be taxed, everyone in his own city.

:4 And Joseph also went up from Galilee, out of the city of Nazareth, into Judea, to the city of David, which is called Bethlehem, because he was of the house of David,

:5 To be taxed with Mary his espoused wife, being great with child.

:6 And so it was, that while they were there, the days were accomplished that she should be delivered.

:7 And she brought forth her firstborn son, and wrapped him in swaddling clothes, and laid him in a manger because there was no room for them in the inn.

:8 And there were in the same country shepherds abiding in the fields, keeping watch over their flock by night.

:9 And, lo, an angel of the Lord came upon them, and the glory of the Lord shone around them: and they were sore afraid.

:10 And the angel said unto them, Fear not, for, behold, I bring you good tidings of great joy, which shall be to all people.

:11 For unto you is born this day in the city of David a Saviour, which is Christ the Lord.

:12 And this shall be a sign unto you; Ye shall find the babe wrapped in swaddling clothes, lying in a manger.

:13 And suddenly there was with the angel a multitude of the heavenly host praising God, and saying,

:14 Glory to God in the highest, and on earth peace, good will toward men.

:15 And it came to pass, as the angels were gone away from them into heaven, the shepherds said one to another, "Let us now go even unto Bethlehem, and see this thing which is come to pass, which the Lord hath made known unto us.

:16 And they came in haste, and found Mary, and Joseph, and the babe lying in a manager.

:17 And when they had seen Him, they made widely known the saying which was told them concerning this Child.

:18 And all those who heard it marveled at those things which were told them by the shepherds.

:19 But Mary kept all these things and pondered them in her heart.

:20 Then the shepherds returned, glorifying and praising God for all the things that they had heard and seen as it was told them.

282. <u>Luke 2.</u> The Birth of Jesus.

Story: A little boy was staring at a family photograph of his family. His father traveled a lot and was not home much. The boy said to his mother, "I wish Daddy would step out of the picture and into our room."

This is what God did in Jesus.

283. <u>Luke 2.</u> The Birth of Jesus.

"God walked down a staircase from heaven with a baby in His arms."

He didn't come as a Giant, stalking the earth, scaring folks.

He came as a little baby that we humans could hold in our arms.

284. <u>Luke 2.</u> The Birth of Jesus.

The pivotal event in human history.

The most significant events in life are often those common, daily experiences seen clearly as blessings from God.

Rev. Jim McCormick

285. <u>Luke 3:4-6.</u> Quoting Isaiah, John the Baptist preaches a baptism of repentance.

"The voice of one crying in the wilderness:
Prepare the way of the Lord, make his path straight.
Every valley shall be filled,
and ever mountain and hill shall be brought low,
and the crooked shall be made straight,

and the rough ways shall be made smooth,
and all flesh shall see the salvation of God."

For us today "valleys" are a metaphor for people who need their lives filled – filled with hope.

"Mountains" of arrogance, abuse, selfishness, injustice shall be taken down.

Rev. Jim Curtis

286. Luke 3:21-22. Jesus is baptised.

"… when Jesus also had been baptized and was praying the heaven was opened, :22 and the Holy Spirit descended upon him in bodily form, as a dove, and a voice came from heaven, "Thou are my beloved son, with whom I am well pleased."

At this moment Jesus accepted his special appointment from God to go minister. It was a turning point. He began preaching. He knows he is the Messiah.

287. Luke 4. Jesus tempted by the Devil in the wilderness.

The "Devil" represents evil in the world.

We are given the freedom to choose, as Jesus was tempted and chose to be true to God.

288. If you want to be miserable just think only of yourself.

Rev. Cliff Davis

289. Luke 5. Jesus recruiting the disciples.

God accepts us as we are, but He doesn't leave us where we are.

290. Luke 6:20. "The Sermon on the Plain".

Beatitudes

Jesus speaks to us on a level plain; where all of us are God's children – all equal in his love: the poor, the hungry, the sad … all of us.

Our goal is to find paths to seek justice, to love kindness, as we acknowledge our connections.

Rev. John Sudduth

291. Luke 6:37,38.

:37 "Judge not, and you will not be judged; condemn not, and you will not be condemned; forgive, and you will be forgiven,

:38 give, and it will be given to you; good measure, pressed down, shaken together, running over, will be put in your lap. For the measure you give will be the measure you get back."

Jesus Christ

292. The more we use our minds the stronger they will become.

Mind, body, heart – use it or lose it.

Rev. Cliff Davis

293. There is an element of chance in life.

Storms will come.

These <u>are not</u> the will of God.

[Gus in <u>Lonesome Dove</u>: "... this is a chancy life."]

Rev. Cliff Davis

294. <u>Luke 6</u>. Jesus choosing the disciples.

Jesus chose disciples because he needed a fellowship: he needed to share; to live with others.

Man needs both solitude and fellowship. (Woman too!)

Jesus needed help in his ministry.

We need help too.

295. The disciples.

After the resurrection, these men were transformed. They were human but these fishermen and common men became uncommonly strong people.

296. Those whose hearts are opened to human pain will see Jesus everywhere, and he will seduce them from that vulnerable place. This is God's hiding place, so only the humble will find him!

Richard Rohr

297. <u>Luke 6:19</u>.

"And all the crowd sought to touch him, for power came forth from him and healed them all."

God can touch all of us, even if we cannot touch Him.

Rev. Jim Curtis

298. <u>Luke 6</u>. The Beatitudes.

These are not "laws".

Jesus instead said that we are to live by spiritual values.

Rev. Cliff Davis

299. Religion can be selfish if we are not careful. We need to be careful not to use God to promote our wants and our ends, instead of allowing God to use us for His ends.

Rev. Cliff Davis

300. <u>Luke 4</u>. Jesus went to the wilderness.

The desert is not a place.
It is a time.
We will be there.
Trust God.

Rev. Jim Curtis

301. <u>Luke 7:12-15</u>. Jesus raises a dead boy when he sees the sorrow of his widow mother.

"… And he gave him to his mother."

Regardless of how one feels about this miracle story, a good point is:

Jesus can help us restore relationships.

302. Jesus' messiahship was in love, not in force or authority.

Jesus realized that you cannot <u>make</u> people be good. They have to do that for themselves.

303. <u>Luke 7:44-48</u>. Story of woman wiped Jesus' feet with her tears, kissed him, and anointed his feet with oil.

:47 "Therefore I tell you, her sins, which are many, are forgiven, for she loved much; but he who <u>forgives little, loves little</u>."

When she felt this radiant joy – when we realize God has forgiven us – we want to forgive others. But the receiving must come first.

Rev. Cliff Davis

304. Part of having the Kingdom of God within us is to be forgiving.

Evelyn Laycock

305. <u>Luke 8:11</u>. "The seed is the word of God."

The more we use our minds, the stronger they will become.

Mind, body, heart – use it or lose it.

306. <u>Luke 15</u>. "And as for that [seed] in the good soil, they are those who, hearing the

Word, hold it fast in an honest and good heart, and bring forth faith with patience."

Jesus is saying: "We need a truth (a truth that will prevail) to build a life upon; and I have come to reveal that truth."

307. Plato: Human behavior springs from 3 sources:

1) Desire
2) Emotion
3) Knowledge (Truth)

"Knowledge should be the pilot of the soul."

308. <u>Luke 8:22-26</u>. The story of Jesus calming the storm. (Rev. Cliff Davis read this verse at the funeral service of Sam Thompson.)

There is an element of chance in life (the storm). These storms <u>are not the will of God</u>.

In the 13th century Thomas Aquinas said, "The providence of God does not preclude chance or evil or freedom."

Gus in <u>Lonesome Dove</u>: "It's natural to worry. This is a chancy life."

309. <u>Luke 9:25</u>. "For what does it profit a man if he gains the whole world and loses or forfeits himself?"

This the <u>essence</u> of the synoptic gospels.

Rev. Cliff Davis

310. God is looking for people who will not only give a helping hand, but who are wise enough to give a preventive hand.

This is why I believe in supporting character building efforts like the Boy Scouts, the Boys & Girls Clubs.

311. Jesus does not persuade us by force, but by example.

312. "Seeking the truth is the intellectual love of God."

Rev. Cliff Davis

313. <u>Luke 10:25-37</u>. "The Good Samaritan".

:25 ... Teacher, what shall I do to inherit eternal life?"

:26 He said to him, "What is written in the law? How do you read?"

:27 And he said, "You shall love the Lord your God with all your heart, and with all your soul, and with all your strength, and will all your mind; and your neighbor as yourself."

:28 And he said to him, "You have answered right; do this, and you will live."

:29 But he, desiring to justify himself, said to Jesus, "And who is my neighbor?"

:30 Jesus replied ... [with the parable of the Good Samaritan.]

:35 And the next day he took out two denarii and gave them to the innkeeper, saying, "Take care of him; and whatever more you spend, I will repay you when I come back."

:36 "Which of these three, do you think proved neighbor to the man who fell among robbers?"

:37 He said, "The one who showed mercy on him." And Jesus said to him, "Go and do likewise."

314. Luke 10:29-37. The Story of the Good Samaritan.

:30 A man going down from Jerusalem to Jericho, and he fell among robbers, who stripped him and beat him, and departed, leaving him half dead.

:31 Now by chance a priest was going down that road; and when he saw him, he passed by on the other side.

:32 So likewise a Levite, when he came to the place and saw him, passed by on the other side.

:33 But a Samaritan, as he journeyed, came to where he was; and when he saw him, he had compassion,

:34 and he went to him and bound up his wounds, pouring oil and wine; then he set him on his own beast and brought him to an inn, and took care of him.

Who is our neighbor?

Anyone who needs help – our help.

315. Luke 10:29-37. "The Good Samaritan".

The central point of "The Good Samaritan" is:

Do good; don't just fail to do bad, but where you find an opportunity to help, do good.

Rev. Cliff Davis

(Nowhere in the Bible is he called "The Good Samaritan"; he is known as "Good" because he did good.)

316. Luke 10:29-37. "The Good Samaritan".

We demonstrate our love of God by how we act toward others.

In the name of compassion, we must be willing to be interrupted. It is risky.

317. Luke 10:29-37. "The Good Samaritan".

1) The robber's philosophy: "What is mine is mine. I use you to get what I want."
2) The Priest's & Levite's: 'What is mine is mine. I will keep it. I'm not going to help you or hurt you.

92

3) <u>The Good Samaritan</u>: What is mine is ours, and we will share it."

Dr. Lukoff per Rev. Cliff Davis

318. <u>Luke 10:37</u>. (The last verse of "The Good Samaritan").

"Go and do likewise."

Jesus: "This is the meaning of life – love."

319. <u>Luke 10:38-42</u>. The story of Martha and Mary – Martha serving; Mary listening to Jesus.

"The only criticism I have of Martha is that she wanted Mary to be just like her.

We are different. Let us be good; but let us be ourselves. This is good advice for a marriage."

Don't expect our husbands and our wives to be just like us."

Rev. Cliff Davis

It's much easier to change ourselves than to change our spouse.

320. <u>Luke 10:38-42</u>. Story of Martha and Mary (sisters) (Martha in the kitchen; Mary listening at Jesus' feet).

To let Jesus into our lives, we need both <u>action</u> and <u>meditation</u>.

Rev. Bill McAlilly

Make room for both the visionaries and the "kitchenaries". We, together, are the community of faith. We need balance.

Dr. John Sudduth

321. Luke 11:1-4. The Lord's Prayer.

"He was praying in a certain place, and when he ceased, one of his disciples said to him, "Lord, teach us to pray, as John taught his disciples."

:2   And he said to them, "When you pray, say: Father, hallowed be thy name.

Thy Kingdom come. Give us each our daily bread; and forgive us our sins, for we ourselves forgive everyone who is indebted to us and lead us not into temptation.

Notice that Jesus' characterization of the Supreme Being – of God – is "Father."

322. Luke 11:1-4. The Lord's Prayer.

In receiving grace (forgiveness), we share it.

323. Luke 11:13.

"If you then ... know how to give good gifts to your children, how much more will the heavenly Father give the Holy Spirit to those who ask him!"

God won't give you everything you ask, but he will give you the Holy Spirit – the spirit of love.

Rev. Cliff Davis

324. Love has no rules; it changes with circumstances; this is the <u>morality of maturity</u>.

****

E.g. Jesus healed on the Sabbath.

Rev. Cliff Davis

325. St. Augustine: <u>Prayer</u> is like throwing a rope to a rock; to bring us closer to God, not God to us. ****

(This is a wonderful, understandable image.)

JR

326. <u>Prayer</u> demands effort. Life demands effort.

We need to keep in touch with God.
We need his spirit.
God may not answer the prayer, but he will answer the <u>prayor</u>.

Rev. Cliff Davis

327. <u>Luke 11:1-4</u>. "The Lord's Prayer".

By praying the Lord's Prayer, we are bending our lives toward God.

Prayer doesn't change God – it changes me.

The gift we receive from prayer is intimacy with God.

328. God's Kingdom is here <u>now</u> – when good is done now.

John Fling – "I don't believe we have to wait to get to heaven to see a little of God's Kingdom right here on Earth right now."

329. We make our rituals, and then our rituals make us.

330. Our most valuable possession is our soul.

Cherish your soul.

Rev. Jim Curtis

331. Luke 12:34: "For where your treasure is, there will your heart be also."

The most valuable possession we have is what we have given away.

332. We need to pray less "God give me _____;" and pray more "God make me _____."

333. Old Hymn:

"My God doesn't move any mountains, but He gives me the strength to climb."

334. God does not intentionally inflict his children.

Rev. Cliff Davis

Quoting Euripides: "If gods do evil, they are not god."

335. Luke 12:48. "Everyone to whom much is given, of him will much be required."

(I have always felt this commission very keenly. Jack Reed, Jr.)

336. You cannot shield your children (or ourselves) but you can, and you must teach them values: what is right; what is wrong; what is good; what is bad; what is beautiful; what is ugly; tolerance; compassion.

Rev. Cliff Davis

337. A good man:

1) Does no harm.
2) Does good.

338. A well religion is love before law; persons before precepts; individuals before institutions. ****

Rev. Cliff Davis

339. The guiding light of a church should be:

"What are we doing to help people?"

340. Luke 13:33. "[Jesus] I must go on my way today and tomorrow."

Jesus is saying here, "I don't have time to worry about, or to be afraid of, King Herod. I've got work to do."

Rev. Cliff Davis

341. Luke 14:11. "For everyone who exalts himself will be humbled, and he who humbles himself will be exalted."

<u>Humility</u> is a willingness to change and to grow and to learn. Humble enough to receive. Not so sure that you know it all.

Rev. Cliff Davis

342. <u>Luke 14:12-24</u>. The Parable of the Great Banquet.

In practicing <u>hospitality</u> Jesus asks us to take a look at our guest list.

My personal motto:

"God wants life to be a party; it's just up to us to make sure everyone is invited."

343. <u>Luke 14:13</u>. "But when you give a feast invite the poor, the maimed, the lame, the blind, and you will be blessed, because they cannot repay you."

Recalls <u>The</u> <u>Mansion</u> by Henry van Dyke.

Its message: don't do good here on Earth for the Earthly good it will do and expect it to be evidence for your goodness in Heaven.

344. People want two things:

to be held and to be heard.

Rev. Bill McAlilly

345. Societies need laws and rules.

Individual need compassion.

Paul Mize, Jr.

346. We are never perfectly whole, but the acceptance of that lack of wholeness is precisely what we mean by holiness, or accepting the "whole" of reality.

Richard Rohr

347. The judgment comes with the use or misuse of freedom.

You reap what you sow.

Rev. Cliff Davis

(Loose living is always more interesting in the imagination than in reality.)

348. Luke 15:3-10. The Parable of the Lost Sheep and of the Lost Coin.

1) God searches for us.
2) Being found is as happy and secure a feeling as finding is.
3) We give thanks to all the saints who showed us the way.

All Saints Sunday, November 6, 2011

Rev. Jim Curtis

(Being on the receiving end of a warm smile is as good a feeling as giving a warm smile. JR)

349. Luke 15:11-32. The Parable of the Prodigal Son.

The perfect personification of Grace.

God is the father.

(a) We are the younger son, (b) <u>and</u> the older son.

(a) :20 "... But while he was yet at a distance, his father saw him and had compassion, and ran and embraced him and kissed him."

(b) :28 "... But he was angry and refused to go in. His father came out and entreated him."

The heart of the New Testament: The relationship between God and man (The Prodigal Son.) The relationship between man and man (The Good Samaritan.)

350. <u>Luke 15:11-32</u>. The Prodigal Son.

Regarding the elder son:

"He never realized the kind of father he had. The elder son was guilty of sins of the spirit. He obeyed the negative rules, but his sins were lack of love, self-pity. Love is positive.

His conduct was correct, but his attitude was wrong. Resentment poisons the soul. Anger poisons the spirit. So, does hatred.

Still the father "came out and entreated him to come in."

Rev. Cliff Davis

351. <u>Luke 15:11-32</u>. The Prodigal Son.

This is a story about a parent who is excessive in his desire to form a family.

Both sons needed the reassurance of their father's love.

God's grace is lavish.

The one the Father is begging to come into the party is you – is I. Whether you are the one who left or the one who stayed.

Rev. Bill McAlilly

352. Luke 15:11-32. The Prodigal Son.

Remember, the Father's final words are an invitation, not a condemnation.

353. The primary revelation of God was Jesus Christ

354. The motivating power of a Christian's life is gratitude.

People who live out of gratitude have enormous energy.

355. Most people experience grace before we give it.

356. Luke 19:1-10. The Story of Zacchaeus (a tax collector, rich, who climbed a tree to see Jesus; :5 "Jesus looked up (and saw him) and said, 'Zacchaeus come down. I must stay at your house today.")

"Jesus never lost his taste for bad company."

Rev. Jim McCormick

357. Luke 19:1-10. The Story of Zacchaeus.

Jesus kept finding people who need him because they are everywhere – in trees, in churches, at your (our) house. If he will eat with them, he will eat with us.

Jesus <u>saw</u> everyone.

Rev. Jim Curtis

358. <u>Luke 19:1-10</u>. The <u>Story</u> of <u>Zacchaeus</u>.

Jesus had the insight to see a human need. Apparently, Jesus didn't preach to Zacchaeus. He didn't tell him that he ought to be in church. He simply paid attention to him and loved him.

Rev. Cliff Davis

359. God is both our Father and our Mother.

Rev. Cliff Davis

360. Jesus is a messiah of the heart.

Jesus was an individualist.

He refused to work out his beliefs by trying to conform them to others.

If we try to live according to others, we are victims of others, and God did not call us to be victims.

We are not called to conform to others.

Rev. Cliff Davis

361. <u>Luke 21:1-4</u>. The <u>Widow's</u> <u>Offering</u>

:3 "And he said, "Truly I tell you, this poor widow has put in more than all of them; :4 for they all contributed out of their abundance, but she out of her poverty put in all the living that she had."

She gave because she loved. As we love, we give. We give to what, to whom, we love.

Rev. Cliff Davis

(Luke appreciated women.)

362. Luke 24:50. "Then [Jesus] led them out as far as Bethany, and lifting up his hands he blessed them."

When we go places and help people on "The Way", we have the chance to meet Jesus along "The Way."

Rev. Cliff Davis

363. By the resurrection God proves that He is ultimate. Evil has no standing in eternal life. It means truth will eventually overcome falsehood; healing will overcome brokenness; grace will overcome sin; comfort will overcome sorrow; life will overcome death.

Rev. Cliff Davis

364. It was not the earthly life of Jesus which transformed the disciples; it was Jesus' resurrection. Without it, there would be no Christianity.

Rev. Cliff Davis

365. The death of the body is not the death of the soul.

Rev. Cliff Davis

366. To forgive is to be powerful.

367. When we weep, let us weep over things that God weeps about: poverty, injustice, people who have lost the best they ever had, child abuse, loss of loved ones.

Rev. Cliff Davis

After weeping,
let it lead us to do something.

368. We must <u>will</u> our future, based on our cultivating of our values. Our values determine our future. We cannot know what the future will bring through the door, but our values will determine how we respond.

(Comfort is not a value. Materialism is not a value.)

Rev. Cliff Davis

369. Re: Holy Communion

While some believe that the bread and wine actually become the body and blood of Christ ("transubstantiation"); and some believe that Christ is present at the occasion; taking Communion is a service to remind us to remember the life and teachings of Jesus.

Rev. Cliff Davis

370. <u>John 1:17</u>. "For the law was given through Moses; grace and truth came through Jesus Christ."

371. God sent Jesus to us to establish our relationship. Then we are blessed by God to be a blessing to others.

(This is one of my favorite prayers: "Thank you, God, for our many blessings; help us to be a blessing to others.")

372. John 1:36. [John the Baptist] looked at Jesus as he walked, and said, "Behold, the Lamb of God!"

Like John the Baptist pointing out Jesus, our mission should be pointing people toward Jesus – the revelation of God.

373. John 21:15-17. Jesus' questions to Peter:

Jesus: "Peter, do you love me?"
Peter: "Yes, Lord, you know that I love you."
Jesus: "Feed my lambs."

Jesus: "Do you love me?"
"Tend my sheep"

Jesus: "Do you love me?"
"Feed my sheep."
Every time Jesus asked Peter if he loved him, He asked him to do something.

374. Be bold. Be great in small things and in big things.

We are God's hands now on earth.
We are his heart, his mind, his feet.
We are breathing for him here, now.

375. Love is also something you <u>say</u>.

    Words are powerful.
    (For good or for ill.)

376. As Christians we believe in daily resurrections: from pain, despair, broken relationships, thru Christ.

377. Difficulty is a normal part of life. Jesus was honest; in the world there <u>is</u> tribulation. But Jesus also promised to be with us, and we will not face these tribulations alone.

378. The cross of Jesus falls like a bridge between us and Jesus.

379. Unlike tennis, in Christianity if you finish up only with love, you've won!

380. The worst things are never the last things in the eyes of God.

    "Never, never give up."

    Winston Churchill

381. <u>John 14:23</u>. "If a man loves me, he will keep my word."

    <u>Love</u> is something you <u>do</u>, not something you feel.

    Jesus' idea of love was the parable of The Good Samaritan.

382. "I can face anything as long as I don't have to face it alone. And particularly when that ally and companion is God."

383. <u>John 3:16</u>. "For God so loved the world that He gave his only Son ..."

   1) <u>Love</u> must be expressed.
   2) <u>Love</u> is strong; it does what the other needs.
   3) The more we give, the more we have.

   That is God's math.

384. Jesus was first a healer.

385. Jesus as teacher – he taught love thru stories: The Prodigal Son, the Good Samaritan, the Lost Sheep.

386. <u>John 4:6-15</u>. The story of Jesus and the Samaritan woman at well.

   Jesus broke the taboos of his culture by visiting with this woman. God's spirit is loose in the world with Jesus.

   We believe all people are sacred worth.

387. Sin always affects the personality.

   <u>Reason</u> is to help us see the truth, including the truth about ourselves.

388. <u>Everyone</u> has something to contribute to the Kingdom of God.

   (John 6:1-14. The Story of the boy who had 5 barley loaves and two fish that Jesus used to feed 5,000.)

3 Points.

1) The boy didn't have much, but he gave all he had, and when it was blessed by God (Jesus), it was enough.
2) He was willing to share what he had with others.
3) What we have to contribute may be exactly what God needs.

389. Just sitting in church does not make us a Christian, any more than just sitting in a garage make us a car!

Rev. Andy Ray

390. When we see the name on the tombstone, for example,

"Jack Reed, Jr."

"October 4, 1951 – _____

it is the dash ("—") that matters.

391. Like a man plucked out of the ocean to be put on an island, we are not saved from sin just to sit there, but we are saved for a life of service, glorifying God, to live a life following Christ.

Rev. Andy Ray

392. The Christian gospel says that the greatest freedom is to commit your life to Christ.

Freedom through commitment. The freedom to do as we ought, to be who we ought to be.

393. "Smile at the people you live with."

Mother Teresa

394. Take time to invest in friendships.

395. Death is a comma, not a period, in the sentence of our life.

Rev. Jim McCormick

396. John 10:10. "… I came that they may have life and have it abundantly."

My personal motto:

"God wants life to be a party. It's just up to us to make sure that everyone is invited."

397. John 11:39. "Jesus said, "Take away the stone."" (Lazarus being raised.)

Jesus needs people to be "stone rollers" to help him bring new life and to serve.

398. At the end of life, we will be judged not by how much we've won, but by how much we've done; not by how much we've saved, but by how much we have sacrificed.

399. John 12:3. "Mary took a pound of costly ointment of pure nard and anointed the feet of Jesus and wiped his feet with her hair; and the house was filled with the fragrance of the ointment."

How extravagant am I in showing my gratitude for all of the blessings I have received?

400. John 14:6. "Jesus said to him, "I am the way, and the truth, and the life.'"

To be a "Follower of the Way":

1) We take the identity as a son or daughter of God; and a brother to each other.
2) We are given a new sense of direction; of growth with other followers toward the kind of world God wants it to be.
3) We are called to a new lifestyle of giving.

Greatness is in serving.

401. We give in response to what we have received.
We love because we were first loved.
We pass on to others what God has given us.
Until we first experience love, we can't love.
We parents need to listen and receive from our children, too.
In listening we are, in fact, giving.

402. Life is both giving and receiving.
We need to be able to receive.
We are not totally self-sufficient.
Relationships, healthy relationships require both.
In order to receive it takes some humility.

By receiving we are saying others are people of worth – that they have something good to give.

403. Our grief is appropriate at the death of a loved one, for grief is the other side of love. The process is painful, but in the passage of time our memories strengthen us. When we weep the death of a loved one, we weep for ourselves. The relationship continues.

404. 1 Thessalonians 5:11. "Therefore encourage one another and build one another up…"

Life's sadnesses come suddenly. No one is exempt from life's hardships. But don't spend your time waiting on them to happen.

Find something good to do.

I aspire to be an encourager.

JR

405. Patience should end when a person's conduct is hurting others.

Revenge is not Christian. Hate is not Christian.

Our purpose is to be good to all.

William Falkner – Gavin Stevens "It's not enough to recognize evil, you or I or somebody must do something about it."

Rev. Cliff Davis.

406. Since we have been blessed, we are to be a blessing.

407. ☺ Humorous Story: A 6-year-old boy is crying on the way home from his brother's baptism.

Q. "Why are you crying, Jimmy?"

A. "Daddy, you said in church that the baby would be raised in a Christian home, and I want him to be raised with us!

Rev. Andy Ray

(Here's a smile for the day!)

408. It's fine to provide our children with physical comforts just don't forget to give them the important things money can't buy: love, kindness, humor, humility, tolerance, compassion, character.

409. Our lives become God's contemporary "word" in our world. If God is in us, how are our lives expressing it?

("By their fruits you will be known to them.")

410. Jesus is the revelation of God.

The difference in reading the word and seeing it in Jesus is like the difference in reading a romance and falling in love yourself.

411. The Book of John

John 1:1. "In the beginning was the Word, and the Word was with God, and the Word was God."

The Word was made flesh. (Jesus)

The Word of God is the essence of God; prior to Jesus it had only been expressed in words.

We Christians believe Jesus is the revelation of God.

412. The proof of the authenticity of our faith is how we love others.

413. A great church's offering plate is full of people.

414. Witnessing.

The question is not will we witness, but how will we witness?

What kind of witness will you be?

How do we treat the hurried waitress who gets our order wrong?

Rev. Jim Curtis

415. The Holy Spirit.

It is the power of the Holy Spirit that sends us out to do the work of God:
to serve at Helping Hands Food & Clothes Pantry;
to prepare and teach Sunday School lessons;
to mentor young people;
to practice choir on Wednesday evenings and inspire on Sunday mornings.

It can be a gentle breeze;
it can be a strong breeze;
but it moves within us to move us where God wants us to be.

416. <u>Acts 2</u>. (Pentecost)

> :2 "And suddenly a sound came from heaven like the rush of a mighty wind, and it filled the house where they were sitting …

> :6 And they were filled with the Holy Spirit …"

The Holy Spirit is God in us. Along side us. With us.
Our helper when we need help.
To encourage us.
To lift our spirits.

417. Paul never knew Jesus, but when he heard about Him and his teachings, Paul realized "this is the way life is supposed to be."

Jesus had a fullness of life. He had the wisdom of love.

Rev. Cliff Davis

418. The closer we walk with God, the more we love other people.

419. <u>Acts 4:36-37</u>. "Thus, Joseph who was surnamed by the apostles Barnabas (which means, <u>Son of encouragement</u>) a Levite, a native of Cyprus, sold a field which belonged to him, and brought the money and laid it at the apostles' feet.

Barnabas is my hero. I aspire to that legacy – as an <u>encourager</u>.

Jack Reed, Jr.

420. The abundant life is following Jesus wherever He leads.

421. <u>Acts 9</u>. Saul on the Road to Damascus.

God is a "God of 2nd Chances."

"Saul", the persecutor of Christians, becomes "Paul" one of the most important of all Christians.

Like a child calling our in the night in a neighborhood for a lost dog, so God yearns for us.

422. We cannot be content to be merely an admirer of Jesus We must be a follower.

423. Barnabas – One of my real heroes.

Barnabas' nickname was "The Encourager". I would settle for that on my tombstone.

To lead the applause for someone else when they have said a brave thing; or done well. To lift someone's spirit when they are low. To give a hug. To write a kind note. To say "well done" and "thank you". These, when performed throughout a lifetime, are mighty contributions.

424. <u>Acts 16</u>. Paul's work.

Paul was helping save people indiscriminately: a wealthy woman, a merchant, a girl, a Roman jailer. He was spreading <u>universally</u> the Word of God.

425. Primitive religions were trying to appease an angry god, who was thought to be against man. But our God is <u>for</u>

us. He wants us to lead abundant lives. He loves us. He forgives us. Our God is love, and He calls us to treat others as children of God, too.

426. Acts 17:27. "… Yet he is not far from each of us …"

Be a bridge builder.

(Kirk as a young girl to Mom and me upon hearing us argue about some trivial matter in the kitchen before supper: "Mom, Dad – build a bridge – get over it!") ☺

427. Romans 1:18. "For the wrath [judgment] of God is revealed from heaven against all ungodliness …"

Sin is a state of separation from God (see the story of Adam & Eve in the Garden of Eden).

Yet because God made us free, we decide for ourselves how we act. However, we do reap what we sow.

Rev. Cliff Davis

428. Romans 5:3-5. "… suffering produces endurance and endurance produces character, and character produces hope, and hope does not disappoint us, because God's love has been poured into our hearts through the Holy Spirit which has been given to us."

A good passage of scripture to remember when the going gets tough. (You have made it through difficult times before; you can make it through this.)

429. <u>Romans 12:6</u>. "Having gifts that differ according to the grace given to us, let us <u>use</u> them."

Not using our gifts is the same as not having them; just as not reading is the same as being illiterate.

430. <u>Romans 12:15</u>. "Rejoice with those who rejoice; weep with those who weep."

There are enough sad times in life. Make sure we enjoy and celebrate the good times.

431. <u>Romans 14:12</u>. "So each of us shall give account of himself to God."

I understand this to be happening every morning when I say my prayers – not just (or perhaps if) at some "final judgment".

432. <u>Romans 12:16</u>. "Live in harmony with one another; do not be haughty, but associate with the lowly, never be conceited."

Actually, there should never be a determination that someone is "lowly". We are all God's children.

433. "Every saint has a past; every sinner has a future."

Oscar Wilde

Religion without grace will crush us as we may try to be perfect, we <u>all</u> need the forgiveness that comes with grace.

434. Ask not, "What is my dream for me?"; but ask, "What is God's dream for me?"

God's future for us calls on us to be better than we are; for ourselves and for others.

435. The God out there in the universe means very little to us in our everyday lives; but the God in our heart means everything to us.

436. When it is proclaimed properly, the Christian faith does not start out by telling us what <u>to do</u>; it starts by telling us who we <u>are</u> – a child of God.

437. Re: Eternal Life.

"The mystery of survival is no greater than the mystery of arrival."

Jack Reed, Sr.

438. How do you get faith?

1) <u>Faith is a gift of God</u>.
   We are born with the capacity because we are born in God's image.

   The Lord is trying to move within us all the time, but we must exercise it, cultivate it, read, think, act, pray.

   The purpose of the will is to focus the attention.

   (We can live in a world of plenty and starve if we don't eat.)

2) Exercise toward it.

Rev. Cliff Davis

439. Tell one who is dying that a part of me goes with you, you will not be alone.

Rev. Cliff Davis

440. From "First Things First"

Physical to Live: nutrition, exercise, control of substances, rest and renewal, financial security, response to pain, live within limits.

Mental to Learn: constantly learning, lifelong education, use gifts and skills, work on long-term development.

Social to Love: relationships that satisfy, love unconditionally, keep (or change) commitments, keep sex and values together, verbal communications, good relationships are constantly repaired.

Spiritual to Leave a Legacy: have a belief system, reach out to others, seek higher than self, stoke the fire within.

441. The Kingdom of God is not without, it is within you.

442. In Times of Grief:

"On death day no resurrection can be had."

Sorrow, anger, resentment are natural human responses. There is a time for them. But we cannot camp there. We must move on to a more whole life.

Rev. Cliff Davis

443. 4 Things To Do In Times Of Trouble.

1) Don't deny them; don't ask, "why me?". Rather accept them, and ask, "What can I do about them?". Deal with them.
2) Take your troubles one at a time and use your very best resources to bear upon them.
3) Share your troubles with some trusted friend. (With a friend yours joys are doubled, and your troubles cut in half.)
4) Share your troubles with God and rely on His grace.

God does not promise us that if we are faithful we will not have troubles. God promises us that in every life situation we are not alone, that He is with us, and He is working for our good.

Rev. Jim McCormick

444. A God that can take a crucifixion and turn it into a resurrection can do good in any situation.

445. <u>1 Corinthians 13:1-3</u>.

:1 "If I speak in the tongues of men and of angels, but have not love, I am a noisy gong or a clanging cymbal. :2 And if I have prophetic powers, and understand all mysteries and all knowledge, and if I have all faith, so as to remove mountains, but have not love, I am nothing. :3 If I give away all I have, and if I deliver my body to be burned, but have not love, I gain nothing."

446. 1 Corinthians 13:4-7.

"Love is patient and kind; love is not jealous or boastful, :5 it is not arrogant or rude. Love does not insist on its own way; it is not irritable or resentful; :6 it does not rejoice at wrong but rejoices in the right. :7 Love bears all things, believes all things, hopes all things, endures all things."

447. 1 Corinthians 13:8;13.

:8 "Love never ends ...
:13 So, faith, hope, love abide, these three; but the greatest of these is love."

448. The best way to send an idea is to wrap it up in a person.

God expressed himself in the person of Jesus. Thru Jesus, God showed us that the world is not a courtroom and God a judge; but the world is a family, with God as a father, loving us.

449. Stewardship.

You can give your money without giving yourself; but you can't give yourself without giving your money.

450. Stewardship: 2 Corinthians 9:6-8.

:6 "He who sows sparingly will also reap sparingly; and he who sows bountifully will also reap bountifully."
:7 Each one must do as he has made up his mind, not reluctantly or under compulsion, for God loves a cheerful giver.

:8 And God is able to provide you with every blessing in abundance so that may always have enough of everything and may provide in abundance for every good deed."

We are challenged to become "money-changers" – changing money into ministries.

451. When we pass on,

What have we passed on to our children?
What values?
How much love?
How much wisdom?

452. 2 Corinthians12:8-9. "Three times I [Paul] sought the Lord about this, that it should leave me; :9 but he said to me, "My grace is sufficient for you ...""

Paul is wise here. Three times is enough, you don't need to badger God. It is not healthy to dwell on your troubles.

Feed your mind with positive, good, inspirational things, great literature, great hymns, great sermons.

Rev. Cliff Davis

And do good things.   JR

453. Galatians 2:16. "... only they [Peter and James] would have us [Paul and Barabbas] remember the poor."

The one request of the leaders of the early church to Paul as he went to preach the word to the Gentiles.

This is the very heart of Jesus' teachings.

454. Grace is the abiding presence of God.

God gives. God forgives.

455. We can't reach out our hand to a neighbor when our arms are wrapped around ourselves.

456. Morality involves not hurting people and enhancing and enlarging the lives of others.

God is with us to help us.

457. Great story!

An Indian chief tells his grandson that there is a battle going on in his soul between two wolves:

one who represents ego, greed, violence, anger, selfishness, immorality;

one who represents humility, patience, love, compassion, laughter, generosity, peace, faithfulness, kindness.

Grandson: "Which wolf will win grandfather?"

Wise Chief: "The one which I feed."

458. Jesus' scars are evidence of his struggles and his love for us.

Our scar shows our sacrifices.

459. The 'rugged individual" is a spiritual adolescent.

Rev. Bill McAlilly

460. If the church is not a home for all, then it is not a home at all.

The church is the dwelling place of the wonder of God Himself.

461. "Consider yourself part of the family"

Our basic needs are:
1) To be loved
2) To belong – to be in a community.

We need to belong to groups that call for the best within us.

To belong to God is to belong to the people of God < to belong to the Church.

With our inclusion in the Church comes a responsibility to make sure others feel that they belong too.

462. We do not obey in order to be loved.

We are loved, and so we obey.

463. We need to follow Jesus not out of a sense of duty but with joy and delight.

464. As followers of Christ we are to be a river, not a reservoir.

465. To use our time well:

1) Make time for growing. Growth occurs best in an atmosphere which does not depend upon performance.

   Every stage of life has its own beauty. Our task is to experience the wonder of the present moment. Don't miss the opportunities.

2) Make time for loving. Nothing compares with a loving relationship.

3) Make time for worshiping.

466. Gift + Passion = Ministry

467. Ephesians 4:1. "I … beg you to lead a life worthy of the calling to which you have been called."

We should live so that when God thinks of us, He will smile.

468. Our daily lives become the grand vision that God has for our lives.

Rev. Fred Britton

469. Our church needs to be, not a commissary, but a caravan.

Rev. Larry Goodpastor

470. Just as a married couple begins to look like each other, we want to deepen our relationship with God so that we begin to reflect God's image for others.

Rev. Andy Ray

471. <u>Philippians1:3-5,7.</u>

:3 "I thank my God in all my remembrances of you,
:4 always in every prayer of mine for you all making my prayer with joy,
:5 thankful for your partnership ..."
:7 It is right for me to feel thus about you ..., because I hold you in my heart."

In my Bible, on page 1421, Lisa wrote this, underlining these verses: "For Jack, I LOVE YOU."

WOW – I certainly feel the same way about her. How fortunate I have been to have the person I love, love me too.

472. Thru Jesus we can define, or redefine, ourselves.

As we redefine ourselves, we redefine our community.

473. Great story about Alexander the Great:

As he approached a beggar, Alexander tossed him some gold coins.
A nearby nobleman said, "Copper would have suited him."
Alexander replies, "But gold is what I should give as King."

My take-away: What we give is more a reflection of us than a reflection of who receives.

474. <u>Philippians 4:8.</u> A great verse. I kept this verse on top of my desk the four years I served as Mayor of Tupelo.

:8 "Finally, brethren,   whatever is true,
                            whatever is honorable,
                            whatever is just,
                            whatever is pure,
                            whatever is lovely,
                            whatever is gracious.

if there is any excellence,
if there is anything worthy of praise,
think about these things."

475. Success should be measured by how we have lived compared with how capable we are.

476. Good story:

A boy finds a piece of a broken mirror. He uses it to reflect light into a dark place to find a coin.

This is a metaphor for us.

We are not the Light (Jesus), but we can reflect that Light and pierce places of darkness, pierce times of darkness, to help others find their way.

477. God gives each of us our boat.

He expects us to row.

478. Relationships are the most important things in life.

Our relationship with God.

Our relationship with others.

479. God accepts what we have been and forgives what we should not have been.

480. Humility, meekness, gentleness — these involve a sense of mutuality.

    A respect for another.

481. <u>Colossians 3:16</u>. "Let the word of Christ dwell in you richly ... as you sing psalms and hymns and spiritual songs with thankfulness in your hearts to God."

    Some of, perhaps most of, my most holy moments have been in our sanctuary inspired by our Chancel Choir at Tupelo First United Methodist Church — of course, seeing Lisa in the alto section every Sunday has made it even more emotional. Singing "Here I am Lord"; hearing the choir sing "Come Thy Fount of Every Blessing" at Kirk and Tate's wedding, and so many more.

482. I am more interested in what your religion makes you do, than what it makes you believe.

483. The smallest act of kindness is better than the grandest intention.

484. Remember, we need to be gracious <u>receivers</u> of encouragement, as well as givers of encouragements.

485. Belief in eternal life is rational, because the best is not finally at the mercy of the worst.

Death will not be the final word.

Jesus' own life says "yes" to eternal life.

486. Jesus.

Jesus was not another Moses; he was not a law giver.

Jesus revealed the spirit in which we should live and make our moral choices. It is the spirit of love.

Jesus' ambition was to give – not to get.

The more served, the greater the life.

487. Hymns that are meaningful to me:

"Here I Am, Lord"
"Hymn of Promise"
"O Come All Ye Faithful"
"Lord Make Me an Instrument of Thy Peace"
"Come Thy Fount of Every Blessing"

488. Forgiveness.

Forgiveness is not forgetting; you forgive in spite of remembering.

Animosity and ill will poisons <u>our</u> spirit, not the other.

489. As we grow older:

1) <u>Keep active</u>. Take care of your body.
   You've got to have it to live abundantly. Exercise, eat right. Go to the doctor. Do physical work.

2) <u>Nourish the mind</u>. Use it.
Always be a reader and a thinker, and a writer.

3) <u>Cultivate your spirit</u>.
With meditation, worship, spiritual thinking, reading the Bible.

Rev. Cliff Davis

490. *3 Principles for Life. (A Life Worth Living.)

1) <u>You've got to have something good and constructive to do</u>.

Examples: *Jesus went about doing good.
*Join Christian study groups.
*Paul, in prison, wrote letters.
*John the Baptist said, "Whoever has 2 shirts should give one to someone who has none."

2) <u>You've got to find someone to love,</u>

*Most have family. (Counselor: Most divorces could be prevented if we treated our family as well as we treat our friends.)
*If not family, friends.
*If not friends, pets. And there are others who need love. The Good Samaritan: he found a stranger along the roadside

3) <u>You need something to believe in</u>. Something to trust in.

Rev. Cliff Davis

491. Biblical Wisdom gives moral insight: what is right and what is wrong. Israel's wisdom literature never distinguished between secular and spiritual morality. If religious literature doesn't help us become better, wiser human beings – if it doesn't bless humanity – then what is it for?

Call me a "Christian humanist".

Rev. Cliff Davis

492. Comparing Judas' and Peter's lives after wronging Jesus.

Judas threw his money back, mourned, but couldn't get beyond his guilt and committed suicide.

Peter denied Jesus, but he moved on, using his experience to make him a more powerful person.

Rev. Cliff Davis

493. Christ never painted a picture, but he inspired Michelangelo and Leonardo to paint masterpieces.

Christ never wrote a note of music, but he inspired the great works of Handel.

We may not know what works we may inspire if we live a life of service and love and joy.

Rev. Prentiss Gordon

494. No place manufacturers goodness like the home.

495. Divine Providence does not exclude chance, accident, or luck.

Christians participate in sorrows; but they should have hope.

Gus in <u>Lonesome Dove</u>: "It's natural to worry; this is a chancy life."

496. Family values.

We need family values taught in the family. "Our family doesn't do this because it is wrong; we do act this way because it is the right thing to do." Then parents need to act that way.

Moral leadership grows family by family; neighborhood by neighborhood; community by community.

Rev. Cliff Davis

(Dad quoted same idea from Confucius.)

497. You don't change someone's mind by arguing with him or her.

498. "Life is lived forward but understood backwards."

Soren Kierkegard

We need good strong memories to use when we look back.

499. God's love is not just a pillow to sleep on; it is a steppingstone from which to step onto to live a complete life.

500. William Barclay:

"If one finds a watch one doesn't reason that the levers, springs, jewels came together by chance. No; one reasons that there must be a watch maker. So, when we observe the world and its order, I believe there is a "world maker".

501. The voice of God is healing, healthy, caring, supportive.

502. 2 Timothy 4:7. Paul – "I have fought the good fight. I have finished the race; I have kept the faith.

1) Life is a battle.
   God does not promise us an easy life; but to be with us.
2) Life is a race.
   Not a sprint, but a marathon. Joy in life is a journey, not a destination.

   We all stumble; we all fall. Failure is not falling. The secret is in getting up.
3) Keep the faith.
   With God's help we can enjoy our relationships with Him and finish the race and fight the good fight.

503. Like the moon we are to be "glory reflectors" of God's glory and purposes.

Rev. Reagan Miskelly

504. The Parables show Jesus' imagination.
All are marked by extravagance.

They have a reversal of what you expect.
And an implied call to action.

Genius.

505. Hebrews 10:24-25. "Let us consider how to stir up one another to love and good works, not neglecting to meet together, but encouraging one another."

"en courage" means "to give courage."

I want to be known as an Encourager.

506. There is no need to put a top on a bucket of crabs because if one crab ever climbs to the top, the others will pull it back down.

Don't be one of those crabs.

Rejoice in other's success.

507. Hebrews 11:1. "Now faith is the assurance of things hoped for, the conviction of things not seen."

I have faith, that with everyone's hard work and passion, I will see a cure for

Jack's Type 1 Diabetes.

508. Will those who come behind us find us faithful?

509. Hebrews 13:2-5.

:2 "Do not neglect to show hospitality to strangers for thereby some have entertained angels unawares.

:3 Remember those in prison ... and those who are ill-treated."

:4 Let marriage be held in honor among all ...

:5 Keep your life free from love of money."

510. <u>Hebrews 13:8</u>. "Jesus Christ is the same yesterday and today and forever."

Jesus   never went to college,
        never wrote a book,
        never made much money,
        never traveled more than 200 miles from home;
        yet He is the eternal contemporary, modern man.

His teachings still provide the best solutions for the problems of today's world.

511. We can postpone our decisions, but we cannot postpone our life.

Every day our lives express our commitments thru our decisions.

512. Prayer.

Prayers of affirmation, praise, thanksgiving.
Prayers of intercession.

Why does prayer sometimes seem to work and sometimes not in other times?

Perhaps the most important aspect of prayer is simply in spending time talking with and listening to God and then responding afterwards.

513. James 1:19. "Let every man be quick to hear, slow to speak, slow to anger."

Complete listening requires slowing down your own talk.

Hurtful words can injure forever.

If angry, be angry over the right things.

514. James 1:22. "Be doers of the word, and not hearers only."

We change the world by being authentic, active followers of Christ.

After reading God's word, ask yourself, "But how can I apply this in my life here, today?"

Rev. Fred Britton

515. If you are strong recognize that everyone is not as strong as you are and don't break someone else. Don't demand something the weak are not able to do.

Judgmental criticism is not the answer.

Acceptance and grace are the ways to make a weak person stronger.

Paul Tillich, quoted by
Rev. Cliff Davis

516. The whole world is waiting on the children of God to grow up and act like it!

517. Jesus was a spiritual genius.

He could receive the spirit of God better than anyone. He was the ultimate spiritual man.

Rev. Cliff Davis

518. Jesus wants his disciples to be great – to be ambitious – to be great to <u>serve</u>.

Rev. Cliff Davis

519. I believe that God is less interested in getting me into heaven than He is in getting heaven into me.

Rev. Cliff Davis

520. Jesus' motive for doing good was simply because it was the good thing to do; it is wholesome, healthy, healing.

521. Yes, religion is a crutch; but who of us is not limping.

Rev. Cliff Davis

522. Temptation comes at us like this:

"Just live a little." "Just this once." "Nobody will know." "Don't be so uptight." "I'm only human."

Then separation from God comes thru the backdoor; and if we give in, little by little, we wake up one day and find that we have lost our soul.

Just as we defend our bodies against heart attacks by good habits of eating and exercise and stress relief, we must defend our souls.

We must embrace God and hold on.

Rev. Cliff Davis

523. It is a great thing to give your life to Christ.

It is a far better thing to <u>keep</u> your life in Christ.

524. Re: the necessity of a conversion experience:

Conversion does not solve everything. It may be a meaningful experience, but a continuous process remains as we continually are responsible for becoming more whole, more holy. In this process we may have new breakthroughs which may be as, or more, radical as any conversion experience one may have had earlier.

Dr. Ted Runyon

525. Young people need to be exposed to needs beyond their own, and they need to be shown that they can help someone else, that they can be needed by someone else.

Jack Reed, Jr.

526. Your attitude can keep you young; can keep you vital.

527. Find something good to do and do it.

Paul Tillich

528. John Wesley's theology:

We are not possessors, but stewards.

We are to use our talents to "earn all we can, save all we can, give all we can."

We are to use our talents to relieve the wants of all mankind.

529. How do Christians handle sorrow and grief?

Learn to accept that which we cannot help. We hope to learn to accept grief within the providence of God. This doctrine (the providence of God) does not exclude chance nor luck, accident or fortune; it does mean ultimate good. (Thomas Aquinas and Paul); that is, working thru grief <u>with</u> God's help.

Rev. Cliff Davis

530. The purpose of life:

Pleasure is great. But pleasure is not the ultimate in life, and it is not God. There will come times in life that pleasure and happiness will not satisfy.

The purpose of life is to love God and to love your neighbor as yourself.

Rev. Cliff Davis

531. "Are you a part of the world's dilemmas or are you a part of the answer to the world's dilemmas?"

Rev. Harry Emerson Fosdick
Quoted by Rev. Cliff Davis

532. James 2:13. "For judgment is without mercy to one who has shown no mercy, yet mercy triumphs over judgment."

The story of "Les Misérables".
A great example of compassion, of love triumphing over the law.

533. James 2:14-17.

"What does it profit my brethren if a man says he has faith but has not works? Can his faith save him? If a brother or sister is ill-clad and in lack of daily food and one of you says to them, 'Go in peace, be warmed and filled, without giving them the things needed for the body, what does it profit? So, faith by itself, if it has no works, is dead."

I am a big fan of James!
Jack Reed, Jr.

534. As we consider we "drink from the cup" with Jesus, remember Jesus drank one sip at a time, day by day. We invest our own lives one day at a time, one check at a time.

Sitting with a person in a time of crisis is a sip from that cup. Teaching Sunday School, singing in the choir, working with MYF are all sips.

Every word of encouragement is a sip.

535. God does not call the equipped, He equips the called.

Rev. Raigan Miskelly

536. Find a way to use your passions.

Remember sustainability is as important as emergency care. Finding a balance is ideal.

537. We don't <u>build</u> the Kingdom of God; we enter it. Jesus is the Kingdom; he is the way. If we abide in God, then we are part of the Kingdom. God loves us; we love others.

I come to church to recharge my batteries to participate in the Kingdom.

JR

It is up to us to be increasing the light in the world.

538. Story of Jim McCormick's grandfather sending his father off to college.

He told him, "I haven't got much to give you. But I have given you a name – and it's a good name."

539. Life is relationships.

Rev. Jim McCormick

We all long for deep relationships.

If we want these relationships so badly, why are they so rare? Because we are afraid. There is a risk in a relationship, because if you don't like who I am, you might reject me.

But deep relationships are worth the risk.

540. 1 John 4:7,8,11-12.

:7 "Beloved, let us love one another; for love is of God, and he who loves is born of God and knows God
:8 He who does not love does not know God; for God is love.
:11 Beloved, if God so loved us, we also ought to love one another.
:12 No man has ever seen God; if we love one another God abides in us and his love is perfected in us."

Read at Kirk's and Jack's weddings.

541. God is love.

We experience it, then we pass it on.

542. Love is the essence of God's character.

God's unconditional love is revealed to us in Jesus.

See Jesus – see love; extended to all the world.

God's love should flow thru us the world.

God ⇨ us ⇨ others.

543. The priesthood of all believers.

A priest is anyone who shows another that God is near.

A great story of a 15-year-old dishwasher at Camp Lake Stephens who "adopted" a special needs kid who only repeated what he heard and was told he would never be cured.

Yet after a week working together, the dishwasher said, "I don't want to do this next year."

"The Kid repeated, "I don't want to do this next year."

"The dishwasher said, "Next year I want to be a counselor."

"The Kid said, "<u>Me too</u>!

** The doctors didn't know the boy would meet at 15-year-old priest.

Rev. Jim Curtis

(On All Saints Sunday 2002, the year Mama died.)

544. For us the living, <u>this</u> <u>is</u> <u>our</u> <u>time</u>.

Thru all the ages, between our father's fathers and our children's' children, this is our chapter in the story of mankind.

This is very inspirational to me.

JR

545. <u>Revelation 21</u>. The gates of heaven:

The gates face in all directions; there's room for everyone.

1) The eastern gates represent entering the church through childhood and growth.

2) The northern gates enter thru reason; cool; thoughtfully; one can have intellectual rebirth.

3) The southern gates enter thru emotion; warm; camp meeting inspiration; being stirred in your heart. (Just remember that you can't feel good all the time.)

4) The western gates enter thru the extreme situations of life; thru tragedy; they realize they need to come into the Kingdom. In these times it's God or nothing.

Rev. Cliff Davis

546. <u>Life after death.</u>

"I believe in life after death. When we believe that the final word about us is <u>life</u>, not death, then our joy is ultimately victory over sadness."

I believe because:

1) Our instinctive longing.
2) My experience with God – a God of love, caring. Harry Emerson Fusdick: 'God is not some crazy artist who goes around painting pictures and erasing them.' Just as I as a father would not plan for the extinction of my children, neither will God.
3) The scriptures promise it,
4) I believe it will be outside of time and space, but I believe heaven will have a wholesomeness of relationship. We will be in relationship with God. We will have our identity. We will have reunion – restored relationships. It will be dynamic; it will be a wholeness of personhood.

Rev. Jim McCormick

547. Grace is God's hand reaching down to you; faith is our hand reaching up to God.

548. The only people we should be trying to get even with are those who have done kind things to us.

We can let our anger grow, or we can let it go.

549. The Family as the Foundation of Love.

3 Points

1) Every family is based on dependable, durable love.

A love without conditions attached; a love without strings attached.

Love is the basic emotional need of the human race; that we are valued just because we are, not earned. The best place to get that kind of love is at home.

Express love for your family when they don't deserve it. Family cares about you no matter what.

Reading to a child is not just learning, it's expressing love.

2) Family values. Our greatest needs are not material. Do we give our family things money can't buy?

Our children are trying to live up to – or down to – our expectations and examples.

Give our children something inside them so that they can take it with them when they leave.

Give time. Give standards. Give fences.

3) Christian homes pray together; worship together; contribute to the church.

We teach more with our actions than our words.

We are teaching 24 hours a day by what we do.

"Toughing it out" without calling on your family for help is to not understand what family is for.

Rev. Jim McCormick

550. Story of Abraham Lincoln:

A Northern woman gave President Lincoln a battle report: "We were victorious: they lost 2500 men, we lost 800; but only 800 mattered."

President Lincoln: "Madam, the world is larger than your heart."

551. "May you be a counselor in perplexity."

(Part of a marriage commission.)

552. Show me who your friends are, and I'll show you who you are.

553. Learn to exercise self-control.

There is a peace that comes with knowing you can control yourself.

554. God can be "the still quiet voice"; but we must be listening.

555. The job of God is already taken.

This fact lifts this weight off our shoulders.

Learn to limit yourself sometimes; learn to say "No" sometimes.

Your batteries need to be charged – and recharged – in order to have the energy to help others.

556. Since there are no perfect people for God to choose, He starts loving us as we are and is ready to use us to do His work.

Thru His grace we become more loving, more helpful, more committed.

Martin Luther: "God carves the rotten wood; God rides the lame horse."

Carving rotten wood into beautiful works, riding the lame horse into this Kingdom.

Thanks to God's grace we can become more than we were.

557. The Spiritual Disciples

I. Inward.
   A. Meditation
   B. Prayer
   C. Fasting
   D. Study

At best thru prayer and meditation (getting to the meaning of our own lives), we can create a sanctuary within our own heart to be with God.

II. Outward.
    A. Simplicity
    B. Solitude
    C. Submission
    D. Service

III. Corporate
    A. Worship
    B. Celebration
    C. Confession
    D. Guidance

558. "Original Sin"

A self-centered life cannot be a God-centered life. Perhaps that is what our forefathers called "original sin". We are set free from our narrow self-interest by realizing that God loves us, in order that we then pass this love on to our brother and sisters of the world.

559. To have the assurance of faith:

We must want it;
we must spend time with people of faith; (it is caught more than taught);
we must stand in the church's places;
we must pray;

we must let go and allow God to give us assurance;
we must act as if God has given it to us;
we must be ready to receive it;
then we must wait .. ,

assurance will come.

Rev. Jim McCormick

560. I love the image of Jesus calling me by name to come join him in the family photograph!

561. Romans 8:38.

"For I am sure that neither death, nor life, nor angels, nor principalities, nor things present, nor things to come, nor powers, nor height, nor depth, nor anything else in all creation, will be able to separate us from the love of God in Christ Jesus our Lord."

"My most hopeful image is, while standing by my father at his death bed, just before he died, he winked at me – giving me reassurance in a moment of my weakness."

Rev. John Sudduth

562. Romans 8:28. "We know that in everything God works for good."

Often that work is done by people who respond to hurt, or grief, or despair, or loneliness – or are there to share the joys.

563. A prayer of St. Francis of Assisi:

"Lord, make me an instrument of your peace.
Where there is hatred, let me sow love.
Where there is injury, pardon.
Where there is doubt, faith.
Where there is despair, hope.
Where there is darkness, light.
Where there is sadness, joy.

O Divine Master, grant that I man not so much seek to
be consoled as to console, not so much to be understood
as to understand,
not so much to be love as to love,
for it is in giving that we receive,
it is pardoning that we are pardoned,
it is in dying that we are awaken to eternal life.

564. <u>Death</u>.

We always hope and pray for healing, but sometimes
healing only comes through death.

Rev. Cliff Davis

565. "Give until it feels like receiving."

I try to remember this and live up to it, particularly
when sometimes I feel frustrated that the poor families
and individuals I am helping don't seem to be rising up
the economic ladder, despite working and trying, and
thus still need my help.

566. I believe our meeting with St. Peter will be more about what we did right in following the Way than about our mistakes.

Jack Reed, Jr.

567. Easter is daybreak.

With Easter God is saying that good and love will live forever; sin and death cannot defeat the love and power of God.

568. "To those to whom love is a stranger may they find a generous friend in you."

(Part of a marriage commission)

May that commission apply to me and to you.

Amen.